NEVER TOO LATE

The trials and triumphs of
starting over at 40

by

Dr DANIELLA T. CHRIS-KUYE

NEVER TOO LATE

First published in the UK in 2023

eBook: 978-1-7394269-1-0
Paperback: 978-1-7394269-0-3
Hardcover 978-1-7394269-2-7

Some names and identifying details have been changed to protect the privacy of individuals involved.
For more information, please contact:

info@chronicless.org

Dedication

To Olu Chris-Kuye, my husband, and best friend.
Thank you for magnifying the highs and cushioning the lows.
Thank you creating the space to expand my wings.
Thank you for walking this journey with me.

To Papa and Mama Mafe, my biological parents.
Thank you for your investment in me.
It was no secret you prioritised my siblings and I above all.
I am eternally grateful!

CONTENTS

ACKNOWLEDGMENTS

"It takes a village to raise a child."

- *African* proverb

The process of writing this book is a testament to the good deal of truth in that statement.

To my second mum–Mama Kuye. It is a hard task trying to explain to people that you are my mother-in-law just because you treat me like your own. Thank you, for your love and kindness always.

Papa and Mama Ashimolowo, my spiritual parents. Thank you for pouring so much into me. Your teachings and guidance were the catalyst that birthed this process of *starting all over again.*

Dr Dipo and Mrs Peju Oluyomi. Thank you for prayers, your unwavering support and timely encouragement over the years. I am deeply grateful.

To my siblings, thank you for having my back and always watching out for me. You are the best gifts my parents have given me.

To my nieces (my royal preciousness)–Fiyin, Rayo and Tiwa. Thank you for being my trusted assistants all through this process.

Oladipupo David–even while recovering from a major surgery, you took the time to review this book and offer your invaluable expertise all through the process of writing this book. You are special.

Ola Nubi. Thank you for your timely advice. I am grateful.

Sola Macaulay of Histiara Publishing. Thank you for your professionalism and for taking on this project despite your busy schedule.

Dan, Del and Fumz (DT's angels). You guys are phenomenon. Thank you for making the last one year one the best in the last five years. You made studying for medicine a lot easier. This sisterhood is a lifelong affair.

To Dr Seye Arikawe, Dr Eugene Ukata and Dr, James Alegbeleye. The first people that gave me the opportunity to experience the world of medicine. Thank you.

Thank you, my host of friends, for your support all through this journey.

PROLOGUE

It was 6:45 a.m. The cold morning air danced in my mouth. I felt my lungs in my mouth, and my heartbeat doubled. I took in three deep breaths and blood ran through my eyes. I raised my head, and my eyes caught the green signal on the traffic light some yards away. That signal undid brakes as cars sped past me, but I couldn't take another step.

I am starting to exercise again after almost two years of zilch physical exercise, except for few movements around the house and the odd runs to catch the train. But, if I must remove the excess fat hanging like tires around my waist, I must continue to release those brakes at the back of my massive thighs and speed off like those cars. I took another deep breath before placing one leg in front of another, and carried on running to the level my body could permit. Fast forward one year later, I can conveniently run 5k.

I tell this story to illustrate how challenging it is to start all over again. It's difficult to leave behind what you know, and it's even harder to build something new that you don't know how to do yet. Starting all over again in life might take a lot out of you, sweat might pour out of every five million pores on your body, and your bones might creak with tiredness. But, if you are to move on from the past and create something new—something better than what you've already done before, it would take blood, sweat, and tears (and more).

I compare my journey in starting all over again to every step I took to burn the excess fat I carried. It was hard to at the beginning, but the more I tried, the more I was consistence, the more benefit I reaped.

I wouldn't say I have been through it all in life. What I can say is that I know life enough to know that sometimes it presents emptiness even as we navigate its path. Sometimes, time itself becomes an ugly ticking exercise that you can't understand. You ask yourself: what have I been doing with my life? That's the question I kept asking myself as I moved from one job to another. The jobs in themselves kept the lights on, placed food on the table, and took me to holiday locations–but they didn't make me feel like I was living my purpose in life. You know what I mean, right? When you're just floating through life, and you're not sure what's happening or why you're doing it? How did I get to this place where material gains defined success and yet, filled me with a vacuum? The memory is clear, but I will not tell it all.

Let's start with a fleshy part. I remember at about nine years old, in Lagos, Nigeria, I was staring at the questions on the common entrance application form. There was joy on one side, and there was longing on another side. As a child, I was happy that I would change another aspect of my growth. That is, I was just an exam away from entering secondary school. On the other side, I longed to dress in beautiful chiffon uniforms worn by those beautiful secondary school girls in my environs. The quest to quickly "belong" among the so-called children who had gained secondary school admission weighed on my parent's minds. And as such, I exhausted my energy filling secondary school entrance forms and battling with the exams at various levels.

That spirit of perpetual elevation on the academic front was the template set by every parent in the early to late nineties. Without an academic trajectory, you were quickly labelled by society as nothing. My parents ensured that I had prepared for entrance exams by attending countless after-school and weekend tutorials. And finally, I was able to get into a secondary school. My closest friends did the same as if there was a consensus that that was our only path in life. That template is still largely at play today. Our destinies are sometimes determined or built with the fond backing of well-meaning parents: education or nothing.

My dad and mum had followed the paths set by their parents and made something of themselves. They too, therefore, saw the need to weave their children tightly into that canvas. To prevent anything outside that would also make them look like failures in the eyes of whispering neighbours. And so, when most visitors come to the house, they would like to tell their friends that their child gained an admission to one right school. To make them proud, I followed their instructions to the letter. Life was incomplete without education, at least in my household.

I had a typical dream. It was to get perfect grades in secondary school, go to a choice university where I would study professional courses that would get me a good job, and eventually bring home a dashing young man who I would settle with for the rest of my life. That was the state of the world in the environment I grew up in, and I could not evoke it in any other way. Doing anything different would have presented me as a failure.

I entrenched myself in the preferences, beliefs, and prejudices of the society. There is a typical dream that every girl must follow–get perfect grades in secondary school. That could then lead her to a choice university where she has to study professional courses that would get her a good job and, ultimately, marry a man and do anything to build a family of another generation of materially successful children.

For years it seemed to me that this existence had become a recurring nightmare. I had followed this path. I landed a good job, settled down with my husband, yet happiness–that light of hope–keeps eluding me. The more I pursued it, the more it departed from me, and this is the story of most people. They have followed the template set by their loved ones, live in the shadows of their past representation, and still feel empty. They keep asking themselves the ultimate question, 'What am I placed in life to achieve?' or 'Where do I go from here?' These are some of the questions that punctured my daily existence. If you have reached this point where these questions wake you up every morning, then I have one thing to tell you: You can retake your life and begin to live on your terms.

James Hollis, the renowned American Psychologist in his seminal book, *What Matters Most*, says, "Until we grow up and step into the large challenge of living our journey as individuals, we will continue to live in the bubble of wishes." I was in that bubble for a while, bouncing around and achieving nothing.

Don't get lost chasing goals and dreams that lead to an unfulfilled existence. The big question should remain: does this path, this choice, make me larger, static, or smaller?

If it makes you static or smaller–if it eats away at your identity or does not expand your capacity (physically and mentally)–then it's probably not the right choice for you.

I know that sounds vague, but it's not meant to be. We all have different experiences and lives shaping who we are as people. So, take this with a grain of salt (or maybe even a whole shaker) when I say: if something makes you feel static or small, it's not right for you.

We've all been there: you're so excited about a new opportunity, a new idea, or a new person that you can't help but pursue it. You're ready to take on the world! But then–what happens? We get caught up in the excitement of pursuing an opportunity, and suddenly we're not sure what matters anymore. Before we know it, we've lost sight of what made us passionate enough to pursue that opportunity in the first place. And before long, we're back at square one with no idea where to go next.

What was supposed to make me larger has made me smaller–and it happens all too often. How do we avoid this trap? How do we stay true to our goals and dreams while ensuring they don't overtake us?

Deep down, the answer to these questions lives with us, but we fear taking steps to be us. We are all afraid of being different.

We sincerely want to be different, but we fear this is not the right time. Perhaps, we have, like me, expended so much of our life living the life prescribed by society and family and don't want to look like a failure to our loved ones or don't want to be the topic of party gossip and saloon chats. We continue to dig ourselves into the pit set by others.

In our minds, it is always easier to follow rather than lead. It is easier to be the sheep than the shepherd. It is easier to be part of a herd than an individual. It is easier to take orders than give them. It is easier to follow someone else's path than blaze your trail.

It's okay to be different.

It's okay to stand out.

It's okay to be yourself, even if it means you're going against the grain.

The world is changing around us, and we can't expect ourselves to be the same as our parents or grandparents were. The world doesn't work like that anymore–and it shouldn't! We need to be able to adapt and change with the times, and if that means being more progressive than our parents ever were, then so be it. I am almost certain it will be the joy of most parent to see their children progress farther than them.

The biggest problem is that we have not asked to find out what's on the other side of starting all over again. At one particular moment, after I had asked myself the deep questions, I came up with the answer almost four decades into life. Yes, you heard it right! Four decades later, I found myself. Finally, I faced myself in the mirror, and those answers I had always known leaped out. I am starting all over with the sole intention of becoming what I want to be.

At forty, many people settle for the daily mundane activities that life throws at them. They attend to the world like one who is watching the same movie over and over again. They know the story, the characters, and how it ends, but can't change it because they are now the movie. I hope that my account helps you to change that movie, to rewrite the features of the character in the film, and, more importantly, inspire you to rewrite the script about your life. At the end of your movie, how would you want to be viewed? Do you want to be known as a character who lived by her terms, drove the plot of the story, and took the necessary action to make the film complete? Perhaps, you too, like me, found out much later in life that there is more to be done than following the dictates of the past. Then I entrust you to read through this book. I don't want to make promises that I will help you climb Mount Everest, but I would like you to journey with me to find out that you can muster the energy to achieve everything you want to achieve.

Looking back on my life, it seems this whole time, I was like a car driven by another human. The driver remained the captain of my destiny. When the configured machines of society and family display a specific type of light, I followed without asking questions because they had become ordinary machines.

I have always believed that the only way to live is to be true to myself, but I was never true to myself. Instead, I let others set up their own rules for me. Even when these rules were broken or unfair, I still followed them because I had become so accustomed to doing so that it felt like second nature. Even those hateful years of existing in the corporate hell didn't serve as a warning sign for me to break the rules for once. I kept slugging it out like a rat chasing cheese in a labyrinth. To unravel the mysteries of that trap, I had to clean up my running clothes, talk to that heavy heart and begin to run my race.

At forty, I started all over again.

Although I started all over again at forty, this book is for anyone and everyone. If your dream leans towards becoming a homemaker, a dressmaker, a baker, an engineer, a nurse, or even a medical doctor like me, this is the book for you.

Starting all over again requires a lot of gutsy attitudes that can't be plucked out of the leaves of any books or from the slippery speech of motivational speakers. This can serve as guide, but I discovered that the true change starts from within.

Determination and consistency were the two most important tool that worked for me. Don't get me wrong; there were moments when doubt sat on my mind like a nasty cold monster. I wouldn't say I killed the beast quickly or used one pill to exterminate this bug encroaching on my mind. I turned around in bed, hissing at everything that crossed my path, and made me talk to myself on the streets on odd occasions. This monster fought with all the positive thoughts that existed in me, but I was able to stamp it out.

I realised that I needed to make my own rules, create my opportunities, and go for it from there. I have already started doing that, and it has been working wonders for me so far. The most important thing about this journey is to keep pushing yourself toward your goal and always remember why you are doing what you are doing and why it is essential to you.

I implore you to take a journey with me and see how I started all over, and maybe, just maybe, you can draw strength from my story.

IDENTITY CRISIS

London—St. Paul's Cathedral—where stilettos, heels, and the wafts of black coffee mingle in one complete union and are blessed by the watchful eyes of St. Paul's beautiful edifice. It's the city where people walked and worked for a singular purpose: survival.

London is a city of dreams. Not just the ones you have when you're asleep, but the ones you have when you're awake. The goals that make you feel invincible, like nothing can stop you, like everything will be okay.

I was living in London, and I had a lot of dreams—the kind that takes up all your time and energy and doesn't leave room for anything else. They were exciting at first. I wanted to travel the world. I wanted to see every museum under the sun. I tried to get into politics or maybe write a book. I wanted to make friends who would be my family for life. I wanted to live in a place that would never change.

Beneath the expensive veneer of London's St. Paul's Cathedral and the beautiful staccato rhythms of fast-pacing shoes, exists unfulfilled hopes, shattered dreams, and misplaced priorities. This is where I got the whiff that I lived in a dangerous bubble. It came in dribs. The beginning was more exciting, and I couldn't have thought it would become a nightmare.

I had worked as a Revenues and Benefit Assessor for a few years before I stumbled onto my role as a relationship management officer at one of the generation Z Quangos established to drive economic growth in London. Some strand of hair still stands at the back of my neck when I think about those years. Daily, I hurried to carry out one singular duties: make management look good–call it a glorified PR officer.

I was a screw in the corporate world's big engine, and that engine screwed me to a fix. The machine promised me monthly cheese and got me hooked on that monthly cheese. During that work, my family and friends had a strange way of always throwing words at me that made me feel like I had arrived at the zenith of a high mountain. 'You've done well!' they would say. But who was I? Who am I now? What did I do to deserve such praise? When did I do it? How did I do it? And what do I have to show for that effort? I did not know what to make of these words or where they came from, but I knew deep down that something was wrong about it all—something rotten and foul! I thought it was an illusion, but one day I woke up feeling like an ant in the middle of a bustling city street. I looked around and saw nothing but strangers walking past me with their heads down, going about their business as if I was invisible. I was invisible–I was just another lost soul that only existed to feed the interest and the expectations of the crowd.

Society teaches you how to remain at a job. They will remind you to thank your stars for being one of the lucky ones. But every time I stepped into the office, I didn't count myself lucky. I felt like I was walking into a vacuum. Every day, my stomach turned, my body protested by placing spots on my face, and invincible tears would wash away my makeup while commuting to and from work.

I went to work daily with the singular mission to be the best out there. In a building decorated with coloured pillars and in a square transformed by fresh garlands, lady luck shot arrows of sadness into my soul. As soon as I stepped into the building, every day, my quasi-achievement floated around my head.

I started my career enthusiastically and with the singular mission to make it. I had heard of black girls like me who put in the hours—got in early and left late—until they got to that board-level position. But, if you had told me that I would change my mind about these beliefs in those days, I would have rebuked you with selected prayers. Or send God's angels to guard me against your meaningless prophecies. You see, we all have a story. And every level has a beginning, middle, and end. If you are still trying to find your place in the world, despair is unnecessary. Here I am, telling you that it's okay to start all over again.

You're a person who lives with a purpose. You've got goals, dreams, and aspirations to achieve.

But deep down, you know that something is missing from your life. You've been going through the motions for so long that you can't even remember what it's like to feel happy and fulfilled. When you're deep in thought, you can't help but feel like your life lacks something. You know that everything around you—the people and the places—is slightly off somehow. It's like they don't quite fit into your vision of how the world should be.

Everything around you seem to wear specks of darkness—but you only accept it as business as usual. You don't take time to step back and ask yourself about your life's purpose or where you want to go next. Sometimes it feels like there's a hole inside of you that's just waiting for someone or something to fill it up. But nobody ever seems to be able to do that long enough before they move on and leave another void behind them. You end up feeling empty and alone again every time this happens. The feeling of pure joy becomes a distant memory from your childhood.

Ask yourself, when was the last time you felt fulfilled? I assure you, most of the time, an answer to this question is: "In my childhood." Because when we were children, we did much more to make ourselves happy and believed that our needs were critical. However, as time went by, the colours of the world lost their vibrancy, and everything became dull–our needs now are lost somewhere in the darkness, rather than just being in the front of our minds, being our priorities.

When I was a child, I was always asked: 'What do you want to be when you grow up?' The idea behind the question is pretty simple. When we know how we want to spend our time, we can determine how we want to spend our days and years.

If you're like me, you probably repeatedly asked this question. You might have even requested it often until you could no longer answer. This happens because the question itself is so broad—it's hard to think about what you want to do for the rest of your life when you're just getting started with life.

But here's where it gets interesting: If you don't find an answer to this question right away, it doesn't mean that there isn't one somewhere waiting for you. It just means that if you keep asking yourself this question repeatedly, eventually, something will click in your head and give you an answer that makes sense for who you are right now.

When we were young, it's easy for us to get stuck in a rut thinking about our future in terms of what other people have told us it should look like. You go to school, get good grades; then you go off into the world and get a job—maybe even two or three jobs—and continue with your life until retirement age comes knocking on your door with a cup of tea and a box full of regrets. Regrets—is this what you want to feel on your deathbed?

No matter how well we do at school or work, no matter how well we treat our friends and families, and no matter how much we achieve in life—we will all end up with death. Everything on this earth will be gone one day—even the sun will die. All our relationships will end one day. Even if it meant we had to spend our whole life alone.

You might wonder, 'why don't people who love their lives keep doing what they love?' Well, there is an answer to that question. They are human beings who are bound to fail and make mistakes during their lifetime (just like everybody else). The difference between successful people and normal human beings is that successful people know how to move on from failure and build themselves back up after taking a hit. They have learnt how.

Don't wait for the post-retirement blues to hit. The happiest people in life choose and create their happiness. They understand what they want and how they can get it. They focus on the bigger picture and not just short-term goals. So, I ask you, 'what do you want? What do you desire?'

For me, my first job began to spring those questions. I began to ask myself if this was it. Even the white walls of the office, the brown wooded doors, and windows in the large office asked me if I wanted to be with them. I recall asking my self over and over with a sigh, 'is this all this is about?'

Smiles left, and depression sat somewhere around the edge of my face. I began to search for other roads that would lead me to somewhere where freedom existed. Days morphed into weeks, and weeks morphed into months. It was during those months that I understood one of the words used most by Dr Myles Munroe—purpose. I interpreted it as the situation we experience when we know what exactly we are here to do on earth and doing it.

The first time I heard Dr Myles Munroe speak on purpose was in 2010. I watched a video of his sermon about how people live to die rather than die to live. He talked about how he knew God was calling him to do something—he didn't know what it was. One night, after another long day and stressful day, he laid in bed with his eyes closed and realised that he had been living his life the same way: waiting for the weekend so that he could do something fun, but not doing anything fun during the week. He waited for the semester to end so that he could go on vacation, but not enjoying the break when it came around. He was tired of just living. He knew there was something more. His message highlighted how our quest for survival fights against our purpose.

This is because most cultures are built around our instincts to survive, to be social and happy. These instincts are hard coded into our DNA and cannot be changed. They make us who we are and guide our lives in subtle ways that most people never notice. They are what keep us alive and well. However, these same instincts can also lead to behaviours that don't quite align with our life's purpose. This creates conflict between who we truly are and whom we need to be.

We experience this conflict daily as we struggle to get by in society while balancing our need to succeed with our need to be accepted by others. We have learned what appropriate behaviour in public versus private is, but it's still challenging to keep that balance when we're under pressure or dealing with it.

Our daily mission is to look for means to keep our bellies filled, pay for those stacks of bills and pay for those fanciable clothes. To meet these daily materialistic existences, we look for the best way to afford these things. Then by doing that, we overlook our central life's goal and get sucked into a web.

It's never too late to redefine our narratives and begin to place the bricks on the path to our freedom. Let me continue with my story to see where this mission to take charge of my life began.

I was fighting in this new hole I had found myself in, but the battle seemed harder daily. There was no winning, except I did something drastic. In thinking about the extreme escape, Kate entered my life.

Kate is London, and London is Kate. She worked in the human resources department in the first place where I worked. Her skin glowed like Ursula Andress, one of the original James Bond girls. If sixty beauty magazines were auditioning for the cover girl of their magazine, Kate would be approached one hundred and twenty times. She represented everything I wanted to be in the professional world—success, beauty, grit, and determination.

That's what I wanted to become, or so I thought. I didn't ask Kate about Kate. I didn't ask if she felt successful in her position or was happy and what steps I could take to become her. I am not alone in this kind of thinking. I have seen a lot of people who have been caught in this kind of mentality. They think they can be just by deciding to be another person. They have not taken the time to sit down and ask if this new being or the person they want to become even sits with their higher purpose in life. I didn't think about Kate's life mission. I just supposed to be Kate meant success. But there was something I couldn't do. I couldn't change my skin to that caramel spotlessness–no career changes could do that for me. Unless, of course, I wanted to bleach my skin which I will never do.

So, what did I do to become that human resource lady in the city? I got some money from my parents to pursue a master's degree in Human Resources. The great attraction for me was not the degree, it was the belief that after the degree, I would morph into Kate. The least forgettable thing about that decision is that it costs a substantial amount to get that degree. I know that regrets and memories are memories made, but honestly, if I knew what I know now, I would have instead collected that money from my parents and invested that money in something different.

I did not have a clear purpose for embarking on Human Resources Management degree.

I completed my master's degree and landed a job in human resources management. I later found out that the fastest way to get a human resource job was gaining experience within the workspace, then probably buttress my experience with a master's degree. Well, because I did not ask questions, the proper steps fled from me. I took the path that has been stitched into my psyche and which is to get things through education.

Again, purpose in life is strewn with asking ourselves the right questions. I didn't factor in some clear things. I was led by what my eyes captured. In fairness to the self, at that particular time, I had not sent my thoughts inwardly to do the tough soul-searching. At that moment, I was still following a script written and deposited inside me. How can I genuinely know whether being a Kate was the right thing for me?

I got a second job in human resources. In that particular work environment, every day felt like I was pouring my life into sewage and drinking pins at the same time. Again, the concept of survival wrapped its beautiful arms around me, and the warm embrace soothed my body. Later, in this place, purpose poked at my innards and forced me to ask myself further questions about my existence.

I would go to work and see happiness oozing out of my every pore. And to cap it up, one time, one of my bosses dropped the N-word on me. He told me I mainly worked in that office because of the "e-ffing diversity policy." I was looking for purpose and fighting against the ugly ghost of racism.

Now, mix discrimination and a lack of purpose, then you know that the end product will be a poisonous cookie. For sure, I can't end racism. No one individual can. It can only end after a long period of unlearning by specific individuals and revamping some of our institutions. So, what did I do? You guessed it. I left that toxic environment.

I reverted to being a revenues and benefits contractor (what you would call a "locum" in medicine) until I could figure out what exactly I should be doing with my life. I wanted to be Kate at one point in life, but to be Kate came with its price. I jumped into her being with my eyes blindfolded. What was worse, I missed the other ugliness that existed in corporate England, which is racism. Every day I was Alexander Wilson, the barrister judged by her skin colour and not by her work. But this book is not about racism, so I would not hammer on that topic. This is a book about starting all over again.

Finding ourselves is one of the essential aspects of our existence. I agreed with David Goggins, the American

Ultramarathon runner, when he said that 'the mind is the first place where the finding of purpose begins.' Goggins went on to say that 'the mind must be fed and watered regularly with information and exercise.' If you feed your mind with negativity and stress, you create a life of negativity. If you provide your mind with positive thoughts and meditate on those thoughts, you can use the power of your mind to overcome any obstacle.

The importance of our minds cannot be understated. If we do not use our minds to find purpose in life, then what is the point of living? One has to be able to ask oneself what exactly one's mission on earth is. If the world ended today, what would you have said you did?

Identifying oneself is pretty hard, but it is accessible at the same time. One of the first steps is taking the self on tour within and seeing and asking the self what it wants to achieve. We know the answers exist within, but we fear the answers. And what do we do? We try our best not to focus on the solutions presented to us by our souls.

Society wired us to think in a particular fashion, to be comfortable with what we have, and not ask further questions about the self. However, that's what contributes to a lot of human unhappiness. That makes us think like the crowd and develop the crowd mentality.

It is a simple thing, yet so many people do not put in the effort to fully understand who they are and what they want to be. We are scared of ourselves. We fear what we will find if we take this inward journey. It may not be that pretty, and it might be scary as hell, but it has to be done for us to find ourselves. And once we have found ourselves, we can start shaping our lives into something extraordinary. It will require hard work and dedication, but it will all be worth it.

I wish I could give a straightforward answer on how to discover ourselves because there isn't one that fits everyone perfectly. But I can tell you this much; there is no substitute for hard work and commitment.

The journey of self-discovery is a process of revealing what we've been trying so hard to hide. One way to do this is to take yourself on a tour of your inner world, and then you can begin asking questions. It's as if you're in a museum with many rooms, and each room has something different inside it. You walk through the museum, visiting each room and looking for answers about who you are and what you want to achieve. The best part about the museum is that you're free to control the direction that you go in.

The thing is, though, that each exhibit comes with some information attached that explains why it's essential. And sometimes, the data can be downright scary—it's just so much easier to remain in the dark about what we most need to know about ourselves. And because we don't want to face up to our fears, we put off exploring this inner world until we have more time or feel more prepared or are somehow better equipped to handle what's inside.

So much of our identity consists of the things that we do every day without even thinking about them; routines like showering or making breakfast or going to work, or whatever else fills up our days. But when the time comes to look at ourselves in the mirror, we tend to forget all of those little things that go into making us who we are. We look only at the big picture and see only the parts that are incomplete, like our hair or clothes or our current level of health. This mindset leads to inner battles and an identity crisis.

Some researchers argued that identity crisis falls under two categories. First is the "motivational crisis," where the individual experiences a lack of guiding commitments and ultimately struggles to establish goals and values. Does that ring a bell? Think about that for some seconds. Do you work to set your goals? What do you value? If someone told you that they would give you a million bucks to sit down in a room for the rest of your life, would you take the money?

The second crisis is a "legitimate crisis" where the person has several commitments which conflict with the person's behavioural imperatives. This is where most of us find ourselves. We know we represent a particular ideology, and yet, we do things that don't meet those ideologies to survive or, to use that ugly cliché, "just to get by."

We are not, as humans, placed on this earth to "get by." We are here for a particular purpose, and the only way to find that out is to do internal questioning. I don't mean to sound cliché, but it's true. You can feel it in your bones when you see someone doing what they love and living their truth—it's like they shine on the inside. And then some people go through life, sometimes even getting by but not living at all.

I think this is because they're just going through the motions of what society has told them they are supposed to do. They're not doing anything new or exciting. They aren't challenging themselves or their worldviews or questioning what society has taught them—they go through life as if they were programmed by some higher power that didn't bother to give them any free will. We can all be Kate, but is Kate's life your desire? Question your place in this world, and you will discover that being in Kate's shoes is not the best possible outcome–no matter how hard your society has tried to prove you otherwise.

When I discovered that I would be miserable living the way that was "socially desirable" and that would make everyone else happy; my quest became to be better at connecting with my inner self. My quest to change the handed-down narratives and the pursuit to impart earth made me choose to start all over again.

THE MOULTING PROCESS

Choose to start all over again–this is the phrase so easy to say but sometimes feels impossible to do. Yes, I chose to change something. Yes, I yielded to become happier. Yes, I wanted to break the toxic cycle of what it means to be "successful." All these "yes," but at the end of the day, I would still go to bed, having no idea how to start this journey and how to put these words into action.

I had been leading a significant corporate life, but it didn't take long for me to start feeling unsatisfied with my life, especially as everything around me was beginning to change. People were leaving; new management came on board; some projects were cancelled or downsized; others launched successfully. As these changes occurred over time, I began asking myself if this was really where I wanted my career path headed (or if there was anything else out there).

Even though I knew there was more to the life I was living, and I wanted more to life, I struggled to effect the changes that were needed to help me. I was carrying too much baggage, and my whole being and psyche needed recalibration to move on successfully.

You know what it's like to be at a place where you're thinking about what else there is in the world outside of your corporate existence. You feel like there are so many things you want to do and see, but you feel stuck because of all the responsibilities and commitments that come with being part of a company.

I want to share some of the habits and beliefs that affected me, and I would like you to think hard–is any of them something you come across in your daily life?

Before now, I believed the way others viewed me was more important than the way I viewed myself: I placed unnecessary importance on holidays, parties, and designer gear often underlaid by shallowness and low self-worth.

Now, I am not saying that you shouldn't have these things–I still reward myself with good holidays and quality clothes and bags now and then. However, they do not fulfil me or give me a sense of purpose. Not like they ever did, but now I know it does not matter if I wear a £1 or £100 outfit. It is what I carry on the inside (purpose and vision) that matters.

Purpose goes beyond me as an individual.

How did I get to the point of having no clue about what my life was about to discovering a purpose to live for? I started by being honest with myself. I asked myself questions like:

Who am I? Not what others perceive me to be.

Do I like the person I have become?

What impact am I making by the things I do?

Why do I earn a decent enough income, yet feel unfulfilled?

What am I passionate about–that thing I can do without being paid for it?

What do I want to be remembered for after I die?

How do I want to be remembered?

All of the answers to these questions can be found in one thing PURPOSE. To put it simply–your mission in life–what your life is about.

But how does one discover their purpose?

I'm sure you've heard the quote by Oscar Wilde, "Be yourself; everyone else is already taken." It's a great way to live your life. Unfortunately, it cannot be easy to figure out what precisely that means. Many people believe they don't have a purpose because they're not entirely sure who they are or their values. But this is not true! A massive component of discovering one's purpose involves taking time to reflect on who you are as an individual and then figuring out how you can achieve your dreams by using your unique talents and abilities.

One of the first things to do is be honest with yourself. Look in the mirror and ask yourself how you feel inside–what are your perceptions of yourself? Are they positive or negative? If they are negative, then consider why that might be so. Is it possible to change this perception through a change of action or thought pattern?

For example: if I perceive myself as being unimportant, how could I change my perception so that it becomes more positive? Perhaps by focusing on what makes me unique instead of what doesn't make me memorable (or vice versa). Or maybe thinking about all the things I have done for others in my life will help remind us that we are loved and appreciated by others even though we may not always feel appreciated!

It can be challenging to be honest with yourself, but it's necessary if you want to discover your purpose. You have to face your fears and insecurities, as well as your weaknesses and flaws. This means looking at your past and all of the negative experiences that shaped who you are today, whether they were traumatic or not.

When people think about getting in touch with their true nature, they often imagine a place where everything is peaceful and quiet–a place where one can find tranquillity amidst nature's beauty. However, this isn't always the case! Sometimes it takes some digging through dark spots before we reach our lighted path toward self-discovery. That's why being honest with yourself is vital: sometimes honesty hurts (and sometimes it doesn't).

Everybody's experience of self-discovery is different. Some start as early as their teenage years, and some start this journey later in life. For me, the journey of self-discovery started when I was thirty-five years old, and I had no clue what my mission in life was. To say age is a function of purpose is a fallacy.

Age is another taboo in our society. Everyone is expected to hurry and create their path when they turn eighteen. However, did you know that your brain is not even fully developed before the age of twenty-five? Therefore, scientifically, it is not possible to have everything figured out before you turn at least twenty-five.

The age factor was a great challenge for me because as the years went by, my hope for changing my life became dimmer and dimmer. My dreams faded away because nobody told me that you could reset your entire life at whatever age you would like to. I have met fifty-two-year olds who had no clue what their life was about, just as I have met twenty-five year olds who had a straightforward course of what to do with their lives.

I started my journey when I turned thirty-five. I realised that at the age of thirty-five, I was not tired because of my age, or I did not feel old because of my age, but on the contrary–I was exhausted because I lived a life that did not belong to my persona. This life I wanted to run away from sucked the energy and the positivity out of me and forced me to age faster. Once I broke through this glass that society suffocates us with, I discovered I was as vibrant, youthful, powerful, and able as I was years ago. I found that thirty-five is too young to feel old, and even more, any age is too young to give up on your dreams.

I waited to find my purpose, and I would not wait any longer. I was not going to try to get any younger, even if people started laughing at me, even if they thought I was ridiculous starting my life all over again at thirty-five. I did not care because I perceive life as the journey of wisdom. The years that are added to our lives gain us one more year of knowledge and experience. Years are so that we can appreciate the road of life we had been through rather than be sorry about becoming older.

My journey to discovering purpose started at the age of thirty-five. Do I wish I had done what I loved since I was sixteen? Of course, I do! However, this was my journey, my destiny, and I had to go through something to discover something more significant, which happened to me at this specific age. So, I must say that I am glad I met my purpose at thirty-five.

Once I decided to follow my purpose in life, I started reading and exploring more through the internet. Losing meaning is very much a global phenomenon. Millions are struggling with this issue of being lost in toxicity. People, who made their dreams come true and worked out the unhappy lifestyle, are always glad to share their experiences with others. So, every year there are more and more messages and books published about finding purpose. Amazon is gladly teaming up with these kinds of inspirational publishers. However, there is not one specific book or publication that is universally helpful. You have to put the time into your research and find out which works best for you.

The two that helped me significantly were *In Pursuit of Purpose* by Myles Munroe and a message by Mathew Ashimolowo titled *The Eagle Believer*. This message impacted my life so much that I spent days trying to purchase the perfect eagle sculpture to remind myself of the characteristics of an eagle constantly. This was almost a decade ago. However, the eagle sculpture remains one of the first items on my entrance mantelpiece to this day to continually remind me of the characteristics of the eagle.

Let me tell you briefly about the outstanding character of the eagle; perhaps you may understand my fascination with the bird and how it has helped me on my journey to discovering purpose. The one that mainly applies in this chapter is the moulting process.

The eagle is not like any other bird. It is a large bird of prey with broad solid wings, sharp curved beaks, and powerful talons. It has an extreme visual power of four to five times better than humans. Eagles are predators–they never eat dead meat and sit at the top of the food chain. They look for and fly into the storm and soar at high altitudes. They can survive in any weather. These characteristics of the eagle combined are a winning recipe for achieving the purpose, which I will come to later.

Like most birds, the eagle goes through a moulting process. It is a difficult period for the eagle when it sheds its feathers, its beak and nails fall off. While on the surface, it may look like a death cross–it is a renewal process.

One of the reasons this happens is, over time the eagle's feathers become heavy with dirt, their eyesight starts to go dim, and nails and beaks begin to wither, and to live longer, they need to go through this transformation. At the end of the process, the eagle emerges with stronger wings, sharper vision, and a more effective beak and talons.

Finding purpose in life is a bit like moulting:

- Moulting is a natural process.
- It's not a one-time event. It happens all the time.
- It's an essential part of life, and it's good for you!
- You don't need to worry about moulting being a mistake or bad thing because it isn't either.

The process starts with the old skin becoming tight and hard to move in, then it separates from itself and sheds off as one piece. When that happens, there's nothing left but a soft new body underneath. The same thing can happen when we find ourselves stuck in our old ways of thinking about ourselves or others. We may feel uncomfortable in our skins because they're too small or restrictive. We may be stuck on thoughts that don't serve us anymore, or maybe we need some time away from negative people so they don't drag us down further into despair.

The moulting process will make you stronger and more resilient than ever before. You will also have gained confidence in yourself and your abilities and comfort with who you are. The process of moulting is similar to finding your true self and being comfortable in your skin. The first step is to get rid of the old skin and be reborn as something new, which can be difficult initially but becomes easier over time. Once you've shed your old self, you will have more room to grow into who you want to be: more authentic, more yourself, and happier with who you are.

I was the bird who wanted to fly into the sky and let my wings soak nature's air. But here I was, too weighed down by the things around me: society's words, my habits, and beliefs, and most significantly, the doubting whispers bubbling in my heart.

I consciously had to go through my moulting process: like unlearning some learned ideologies. For example, education is the gateway to an all-purpose life. I have discovered that that's not true–says a woman with three university degrees. Sometimes the best way to get to your destination might not necessarily be through the route of an institution.

I also had to unlearn that having money itself is not a guarantee to happiness. It is the impact you make with the money that brings greater joy. If you doubt this, I implore you to listen to Viola Davy's interview with Oprah (2022).

I preached about my purpose to those who I thought were my close friends, but they laughed and waved at my dreams like I was a pariah. They would ask how someone my age would talk about a career change, especially in the medical field! They laughed, but I never allowed their laughter to create a hole in my heart.

In their eyes, I was on the wrong path. And to be honest, they meant well, but I knew what I saw, and I knew how I was going to get there. Something, however, did happen when I began to delve deeper into what it took to be successful in the medical profession. I discovered the amount of work required, and I started to hang out less, holidays reduced, needless dinners halted, and I noticed some individuals fall off like lousy fat on the body of a training athlete.

When you are elevating to a new space, some things have to fall off. In other words, for you to go up, some things must fall. If I don't let go of all those past stories, my flight to this new purpose will be affected. The best thing I did was for me to focus on the things ahead. Sometimes when these thoughts became too heavy, I used them as fuel to push me to where I am going now.

The pursuit of purpose will lead you to a spot where you have to reassess all your beliefs. Every belief, as Jordan Peterson argues in his book *12 Rules for Life*, is either fed to us or learned and so we must question these beliefs as we evolve. There is that moment when the mountain you've always wanted to climb will come to you, and at that point, there is no other option for you to train for the mountain climb. Before climbing any mountain, any mountain climber knows that she must be in optimal shape and know the correct type of food to eat to reserve energy when climbing those treacherous mountains. Ask Ant Middleton, the British adventurer who climbed Mount Everest, and he will tell you that you can't take a lot of things with you when trying to reach the mountain tops, and he will tell you that you must control your steps on some paths.

Let's assume that a captain is on a sea sailing onto another land. Then on one of his screens, he notices that the ship begins to sink in one area. Upon investigation, he discovers that some goods are pulling the boat. What do you think he will do?

There is a moment in your life when you must take stock of what is pulling you back. You must, like the captain, be able to take serious stock of the things in your life. If you want to be a good parent, you must assess how you've done so far and take the necessary steps to become better. If you're going to be financially free, you must consider what is holding you from reaching that desired freedom. When you locate these things, you must ruthlessly offload these things.

For me, I took stock of all my strengths, weaknesses, and everything in between. I knew it was hard for me to gain the illusion of happiness from a job, and I realised that boredom crept into my being every time I worked in these beautiful buildings. I usually would turn into a zombie and drain into depression. Another thing I realised is that I am often quite energetic when it comes to helping people become a better version of themselves. I took some days out to write out what exactly I have strengths in, and the discovery was quite impressive.

You might think what worked for me might not work for you. And you might be right. However, there is one thing that is constant in our lives. Being stuck in an endless loop of working without a purpose is like living in a trap. It's a metaphoric death. It is what Dr Myles Munroe, in his book *In Pursuit of Purpose: The Key to Personal Fulfilment*, describes as "The greatest tragedy in life." To avoid that tragedy, therefore, it is essential to living a life with purpose, to empty ourselves onto earth and bless the world with our gift.

For me, I believe the most challenging step towards pursuing any purpose is taking that first step–asking yourself what your life is about. Would you take that first step?

Having a sense of purpose in life can be one of the most rewarding things. Once you know your goals in life, you will feel like there is a meaningful reason for every step you take on this earth. Purpose gives you drive; it gives you passion and hope.

I think many people have lost their purpose in life because they have lost touch with what they love to do. They are working at a job that they feel like they need to work at instead of working at something they want to work at. They feel obligated to spend time with family and friends instead of spending time with them because they love them. They live in a place that is not their home; it's just where they live now.

To find your purpose in life, you must get back in touch with what drives you and makes your heart sing. What makes your heart sing could be anything. It could be helping others or creating art or writing literature or being alone and peaceful or running around outside or helping animals, or being social and friendly. Anything that makes your heart sing is what can give you the motivation to seek out your purpose in life and follow it through

I am not saying that asking the question would immediately morph you into the next Oprah Winfrey. I am saying it can serve as a springboard to finding purpose. There are no right or wrong ways. And there is no definite number of days for you to find meaning. It would be best if you kept searching.

And to be fair, some people's purpose in life might be the nine-to-five daily grind which is not a bad thing in itself. I remember Naomi, who ensures our house remains spick and span always. There is a military method to Naomi's professional delivery. It was as if when she walked into our home, every dust kowtowed to her and obeyed her commands. I don't know how she does this, but she has become her job. She is a no-nonsense individual and maintains a tall focus when carrying out her duties. If Naomi were in charge of earth's cleanliness, I am sure it would look romantic. She aims to ensure that she is one of the best housekeepers and doing a marvellous job. I think what makes her distinct is she is proud of her work, and she can pour herself into it without paying attention to time.

The concept of finding yourself is different for many people. Not all of us can be Naomi. But all of us can discover why we are here. It's a bad thing to allow our existence to be based mainly on survival. I know it is a moot point, but it is what I believe. Looking solely at survival might be the digging of our graves.

One thing that I like to do when I feel a little blue and a little lost is to think about what I want my life to be. I don't mean in five years or even in forty years. I mean in five minutes or even in forty minutes. Not just what will happen, but who am I right now? What is my purpose right now? A lot of us have jobs we don't like but feel trapped because we don't know what else we could do that would make us happy. Maybe you know what you want to do for a living, but you are sceptical or doubtful. You are not alone. Some of the greatest people of all time notably George Washington and Abraham Lincoln struggled with tremendous fear and self-doubt, however they learnt to manage their fears and doubts and firmly carved their footprint on the sands of time.

You can start with baby steps.

Today, seek to do things that would change one person's life. It might be as simple as putting a smile on someone's face through thoughtful action. See how that makes you feel. Each of us has a particular reason for being here–not only on a grand scheme but also on a daily scale. We each have something that makes us special and unique. We are here to learn, share, experience life, and help those around us. I believe in a big picture approach, that everything is intertwined like some giant quilt or tapestry. Everything happens for a reason, and our lives are meant to be lived well.

When you look at the world around you from this perspective, it will change your life. You will look at people differently, and you will treat them differently because you know that everyone is here for a reason, even if they don't know it themselves. You will look at the homeless person on the street as someone who isn't lost by choice. You will look at the rude cashier as someone struggling with something. You will see your friends as valuable people who are so much more than just friends. You will see yourself differently when you acknowledge that there is no such thing as coincidence in this world.

There are times when the purpose will come disguised as something uncomfortable. Take the time to pay attention to it. Probe it. Examine it. Go through your moulting process.

Do you honestly believe that you should exist as a human being on this earth without leaving a mark? There is a part of the Bible that resonates with me in Genesis 1:28, where God talked about us having dominion over everything around us. If you don't want to look at it from the religious point of view, you can argue that until you decide to take your own up and live a purpose-filled life, you will live a borrowed life.

I believe that there is no one in this world who doesn't want to be the best version of themselves. All of us strive to live our lives to the fullest and feel that it is fulfilling, regardless of our circumstances or our past. We sincerely desire to live life purposefully, striving for what we love and controlling the things around us. But sometimes, it seems like our lives are controlled by other people. We're stuck in situations with no way out or in places that we don't even want to be. It's hard to focus on being happy when so many things take away from our happiness.

But before you can begin moving forward, you must learn to let go of everything holding you back. You have to learn how not to let the past drag you into the future. It's okay if you feel like your life is a mess. It's okay if you feel like everything is falling apart. It's okay if you feel like this might be too big for you, but if you can dare take time to thoroughly assess your life–look at your fears and weaknesses in the face and identify what areas of your life needs rekindling: relationships, finances, health, or careers? Then consistently take small actions toward your desired goal. I promise you will inevitably reap the benefits; just like the story I shared with you at the start of the book.

The secrets of champions are determination and consistency.

The moulting process, therefore, is a combination of taking stock of what holds us back from achieving what we want to accomplish and sitting down to calculate how we can reach our destined goal.

I was fortunate enough to know that my life is much more than scraping some office tables with files and pens to survive. I found that in the direct service of other people, I can become my whole self and much more.

Recently, I was talking to a friend, and I asked her what she thought the real meaning of purpose is. She said she had not thought about it and she doesn't want to bother about those types of philosophical reasoning. Some of us are in that position where we don't want to confront that question. We wish to coast because it is safe, and everyone is doing that. But how can we know if we don't attempt it? How can we live fully without fulfilling the true meaning of purpose?

Sometimes, I look at the lives of those who truly live their purpose, and I have realised that it is much more than money. What inspired someone like Martin Luther King Jr. to sacrifice his life for black liberation? Was he paid for that purpose?

What inspired Mother Theresa to live a life where her existence depended solely on giving her life for the betterment of others? I don't think the financial return inspires these heroes. These heroes died pennilessly but tremendously changed the world.

Although I believe purpose should come with some financial rewards enough to live a decent life. I believe purpose, therefore, means looking for that act that will change the world. It means searching for what will inspire change and impact the lives of others. It means being part of something bigger than yourself and finding happiness in knowing you are making a difference in someone else's life or simply making their day better by being kind to them or helping them out when they need it most.

When I think about my own life, I know that many things have inspired me to make a difference in the world: family, friends, music, arts, traveling, people doing good deeds without recognition or reward, and nature itself. These are just some examples of things that have inspired me over time. And now, I want to share this inspiration with you!

Purpose is found in our passion for serving others. Rather than seeking personal gain or fame, it is about living a meaningful life and improving the world, and sometimes the process happens naturally through trial and error (or maybe even failure).

I don't want to sound too religious, and I hope this book doesn't portray that. But it is indeed spiritually uplifting, regardless of what you believe in, to find your life's purpose.

I must add before concluding this chapter that when I discovered my purpose, which is to bless the world with my greatest gifts (care and compassion) by serving in the medical sphere, I began to notice that there were other potentials within that field. I began to think of new ways to cater to people's minds through writing and hosting book clubs where I share lessons from books I have read. Once you discover purpose, the willingness to serve the world becomes natural.

Not to sound like a self-tooting machine, let me continue with how I dropped everything and deviated to the medical line. The journey began when I consciously went through my moulting process, took stock, and finally saw the purpose of my existence on earth. The trip was indeed a bumpy ride. Let's continue, and I can only tell you to hold on tight.

REINFORCE THE VISION WITH A DECISION

I am a firm believer in tempering, as well as tempering with intent. Understanding the temperament process is a lifelong journey. During moulting, I assessed, analysed, and processed my temperament, skills, strengths, weaknesses, likes, and dislikes. I became more intentional with my actions. More importantly, I worked hard at answering those questions in Chapter two. The journey of self-reflection is a lifelong one that helps us grow into the best versions of ourselves by helping us understand what we want out of life and how we can achieve those goals by working hard toward them every day.

As I went through moulting, I became more intentional with my actions. I became aware of what was happening and how it affected me. I started to notice the impact of my words on those around me. I began paying attention to what made me happy or sad, which allowed me space from negative thoughts that might otherwise have consumed all of my time if left unchecked.

At the end of the process, I discovered some new truths about myself, which guided me to change my career into healthcare. I found that my greatest gift is care and compassion.

I am passionate about lifestyle medicine. Anyone that knows me well will know how much I have preached about healthy eating from a very young age, even without knowing I would end up in health care.

- I have a curious mind and have always been fascinated by the physiology of the human body.
- I could not be in a profession deficient in high-level human interaction.
- I enjoy intellectually stimulating activities and conversations.
- I get job satisfaction from direct contribution/ decision-making/problem-solving.

The discovery helped match my personality, strengths, weaknesses, likes, and dislikes to the type of business or career that I may be suitable for and narrowed it down to:

- Entrepreneur
- Post-secondary teacher
- Social work
- Business analyst
- Project management
- Seamstress
- Interior decorator

- Health care professional (This could have been a nurse, midwife, health care assistant, dentist, or medical doctor.)
- Nutritionist
- Dietitian

I quickly ruled out the business/jobs I could or could not do, even if I was paid a million pounds to do them.

I narrowed my options to health care; it was most suited to my natural capabilities, personality, likes, and dislikes.

This left me yet with more questions:

- How do I start a new career at thirty-five years old? And at what cost?
- How would my husband and I cope with the drop in household income if I go into full-time education?
- How would this affect my marriage?
- How would my tuition fees be funded? As of the time I am writing this, the UK government does not support you with tuition fees if you have a degree prior to starting medical school.

The healthcare profession offered me many options that left me at a crossroads.

I spent time exploring each career option and researching the requirements. I talked to people who had done each option, made a list of pros and cons, and then took a step back to look at my options from a broader perspective.

I realised that there were things I liked about all healthcare careers. They all involved working with patients or clients in some way (which was essential to me), and the healthcare professions allowed me to help others as part of my job description (another priority).

I did not want to make the same mistake I did in assuming being Kate, the HR officer, would fulfil my career. So, this time I prayed for guidance. I prayed not to get it wrong. I prayed until I had the peace that Health Care Profession was the right path.

I spoke to nurses, dentists and medical doctors, dental and medical students at different stages of their careers, and I asked questions.

Ironically, most of the junior doctors I spoke to discouraged me from pursuing a medical career–I don't blame them. This was at the time when junior doctors were at loggerheads with the then health secretary–Jeremy Hunt–and a lot felt under-appreciated and fed up with the profession

This is why it is essential to be sure of your vision before you put it out there so it does not get drowned out by other people's doubting voices.

Healthcare comes in various categories–I had to think about which was perfect for me. I was torn between general nursing, dentistry, or medicine. I decided to take on work experiences to have a first-hand experience of work in the health sector.

Work or volunteer experiences in healthcare would not only give you an edge in applying to dentistry or medicine–it would also show proof of your commitment to study dentistry or medicine. And proof that you made an informed decision–that you are well aware of the work involved in dentistry and medicine.

I sent countless work experience request emails to as many dental practices within my locality as possible (possibly about fifteen) but received no response. I followed up in person, and the feedback was the same, almost like a memo titled *Avoid DT Chris-Kuye* had been circulated within my local dental community.

I remember going to one of the dental practices. I walked into the neatly decorated, well-lit reception in a refurbished detached Victorian house and met a lady who I believed was doubling up as a dental nurse/receptionist. I gave her a brief narration of my story, of how I am a prospective dental student seeking work experience. I had sent an email before my visit and decided to follow up as I did not hear back.

'Are you sure you want to be a dentist or a dental nurse?' she responded in a West African accent.

'A dentist, sis,' I responded to her in an accentuated West African accent to establish a connection. She raised her head from whatever was hidden behind the tall reception desk that kept her eyes away from me when she talked to me. She gave me a look that expressed a facial expression of disapproval for a few seconds before blurting out, 'You need to be more realistic,' exposing the gap between her coffee-stained central incisors wedged between her badly painted red lips.

I was going to respond to her by saying your employer is doing a lousy job in using your teeth as the patent's first encounter, and secondly, you do not have good enough friends to tell you to fix your teeth, but I was too stunned to do so. Her words reverberated through my ears to my brain and down my spine. My tongue felt glued to the roof of my mouth, just like my legs felt glued to the ground, for I don't know how many seconds or minutes, but what seemed like an eternity. I was drained of enthusiasm and optimism.

All I managed to muster was, 'Oh, okay,' and I dragged my limp 56kg body out of the surgery, not before looking around to see if anyone in the waiting area had overheard our conversation. No one seemed to have noticed, or perhaps they did but were too occupied with the terror of being in a dental surgery.

Eventually, I was introduced to a dentist in my church community who willingly took me under her wing to gather work experience enough to help my application to university. Her surgery was about twenty-seven miles away from my house, so alongside my full-time job, I ended up doing six months of unpaid dental work shadowing. I condensed my working hours to four days, so I worked ten hrs/day over four days a week and spent one day a week at her dental surgery.

Not only did she allow me to explore my dream, but she also opened my eyes to the endless possibility of what it can be when you choose to follow your dream. She shared her experience of taking a break from dentistry to raise her children. She returned after sixteen years to a more challenging terrain than she knows, but she persisted. She failed her exam twice before passing on the third attempt, and for years she worked away from home and would only return at the weekend. She eventually opened her surgery.

This lady and her husband, a doctor, have cheered me on since I shared my dream with them. I am very grateful to them and will forever hold them dear. My peak moment happened within my six months of work experience as a dental work experience student. I had gathered a little, but enough insight to know dentistry was not for me. I am interested in broader health concerns, not just oral diseases.

I am more interested in acute medicine and preventative/ lifestyle medicine, i.e., how can I stop this person from bleeding to death, or how can I help this person lose weight, to prevent them from having heart disease or diabetes? How can I help somebody to stop smoking to avoid lung cancer, etc.?

It was challenging to get work experience in an emergency department. However, I secured work experience at an elderly ward through Dr W.A, a consultant in my local church. He was so impressed at the decision that he took me into his community.

This was a real eye-opener to the world of medicine. It was here I first experienced ward round. It was here I first encountered the hierarchy that exists in medicine. It was here I first experienced how to treat a patient holistically. It was here I first experienced the importance of a multi-disciplinary team (MDT).

One of the saddest experiences of my work in the elderly care ward was a patient I got fond of in this community. I left him well enough the day before, and the day after, I was in the mortuary with a junior doctor inspecting his chest for a pacemaker. While I was sad about the passing of my beloved Mr. T, I was impressed I could withstand the site of countless dead bodies.

I also approached a GP surgery manager–one of the most kind-hearted ladies I knew–her name was Lou. She managed the GP surgeries next to the building I was working in at the time. She arranged work experience for me at her surgery. My takeaway message from the GP work experience was how not to be an arrogant doctor. I learned the power of listening to patients. Listening to patients is paramount. It's not just about listening; it's about hearing. And it's a skill that can be learned.

Listening will help you understand your patient better, which means you'll be able to make better decisions on how best to treat them. Listening helps them feel more comfortable in the consultation room, and they will trust you more as a result. Trust is an essential factor in any relationship between doctor and patient. I knew that as a doctor, I would work with many different kinds of people. I needed to communicate with them effectively and show interest in their lives.

If you are too arrogant or a know-it-all, patients will not trust you enough to open up about their problems and situations. They may also feel like they cannot ask questions because they do not want to look or feel stupid. Patients should feel comfortable asking questions without feeling judged by their doctors, and that starts with how those doctors themselves act.

While working as a GP, I saw many patients and learned that they are not just numbers. They're human beings who deserve respect and empathy. The way you treat your patients is essential because it can affect how well they do in treatment, whether or not they come back for follow-up appointments, and whether or not they recommend their friends or family members to see you as well. At the end of both medical experiences, I was sure I could become a doctor.

I have often heard that you do not need too many people in your boat to succeed, and at the same time that it takes a village to raise a child. Juxtaposed? I had both experiences in my journey of starting all over again

In my starting all over again, I got help from the people that mattered–the person who introduced me to the dentist, the dentist and the consultant that I mentioned. I was deeply hurt and rejected by those that did not believe I could birth the vision. This rejection and disappointment that were more difficult to shake off came from close people I relied on–some had promised to connect me to secure dentistry experience in a surgery or hospital. Most stopped picking up my calls or responding to my messages when I tried to make contact for updates on the help

I needed, which gave me an incline of how Jesus must have felt when betrayed by Judas Iscariot.

I recalled sharing the dream of studying medicine with a friend who said, 'But you do not come across as someone who could become a doctor.' I remember another one who asked, 'How many careers do you want to have in a lifetime? All you need to look for now is money.' Most said to concentrate on starting and raising a family.

I also did not share the plan with my mother until almost the end of my first year in Medical school, this is because the only vision she saw for me at the time was to bear her grandchildren. No doubt she would be happy and supportive, but she would have been happier if I diverted all the energy to getting pregnant.

I shared this with you to say when you are doubly sure you have made the right decision; when you are sure of the direction you need to travel, never be afraid to walk alone. At some point in our lives, we all walk alone. We cannot always depend on others to help us through the challenges that life throws at us. Sometimes, we must learn how to cope with problems by ourselves. And sometimes, we need to be able to make our own decisions without depending on others' advice or opinions even if they're good ones. The fear of being alone is a natural human emotion. It is the fear that you will be unable to cope with or overcome a situation. This can lead to depression, anxiety, and even suicide in extreme cases.

I have learned that no matter how much you think about things beforehand, sometimes life throws you curve balls that make everything seem impossible at first glance. But if we look closely enough at these challenges, we will see that there are ways around them if we just put our minds into action–if we find our purpose.

UNDERSTAND YOUR WHY AND TAKE ACTION

The difference between doing and being is between living a life that matters and simply existing. If you want to be more than just a cog in a machine, if you want to find your purpose in life, it's time to start thinking about what makes you tick.

My motto is "Take Action!" because I believe in taking action over sitting around waiting for something good to happen. In this post, I'll explain why "taking action" means not only putting yourself out there but also understanding why you do what you do: your purpose.

Many things make people act. However, we must always think about the why. In Simon Sinek's book, *Start with Why: How Great Leaders Inspire Everyone to Take Action*, he reminds us that the beginning of greatness starts with looking inwards and digging out the reason why we want to achieve a particular goal and goes further to give examples of how great companies like Apple have been able to remain great over the years. However, looking at the book's premise, I think this can be applied in our day-to-day life. Without looking into why we are doing what is expected of us to do, we would maintain a wild dream, and mostly this would lead to depression and following the crowd.

To take action, you need to know your why. Your why is why you got into this business in the first place and what keeps you going even when things get tough. It also helps keep your focus on what matters most: helping others.

It could be as simple as 'I love helping people,' or something more complex like 'I want to give back after my parents passed away by helping others who have lost someone important in their lives.' In either case, we all need to understand our true purpose and know our reasons for doing what we do or what we want to do and to use those motivations as fuel for taking action every day.

This is the difference between having a job that pays you money and having an experience that makes you happy daily. This is choosing to live in service to others instead of serving yourself first.

It means you're comfortable being uncomfortable because it allows growth opportunities, and growth opportunities lead to betterment in all aspects of your life. However, taking action means that you may fail–it is inevitable. You must learn how to get back up and continue doing your best to become YOUR best.

I've always prided myself on being a strong woman. However, life–the unpredictable flows of reality–is designed to throw stones at our rivers of existence to test our flow. Everyone, regardless of race and gender, will have their tests. Every time we hit a wall, every time we're at the end of our rope, and there's no way forward, every time life wraps its knuckles around our throat and screams for attention–it's easy to look back at the past to see where the path went wrong. It's not hard to find fault–if we just hadn't done this or that, then maybe we wouldn't be in our current situation. If only we had made a better decision or said something different. But even if we could go back and change it all, would it make any difference?

The world has a way of turning us on our heads with an unfairness so blatant that it leaves us wondering why we even bother getting out of bed anymore. But that doesn't mean there isn't a reason for us getting up each morning or that we're not capable of pulling ourselves back up again.

What matters is how we receive the blows of life's stone and keep moving.

Let's start with a story.

One day, I was happy to celebrate two significant things–first, my birthday, and second, my admittance into the university to study medicine. I felt like I was on top of the world, and nothing could bring me down.

In between these two joyous occasions, I had a miscarriage. The news came on a calm summery day. As life went on, I realised that the miscarriage was one thing that made me happy and sad at the same time. I suffered from headaches and unending salty tears.

The aftermath of the miscarriage was killing me inside. It felt like someone was ripping my heart from my chest and tossing it in a blender. Through all that pain, I still wanted to help others with their suffering, but how can you do that when you're suffering yourself?

But then again, who am I to judge? Life is not fair to all of us. This whole journey called life is just like a roller coaster ride where we experience ups and downs. But in any roller coaster ride, there are only three options: get off, stay, or go again, trying to reach new heights and lows.

I wanted everything to be different. I liked the three news to be good. But life doesn't always go the way we plan it to be. It flows, and there are stormy times, and there are smooth times. The question remains how one will handle them. This was not all.

The problem for me was that I was too focused on the outcome of my educational pursuit. Because I had fallen deeply into the higher calling to becoming a doctor, it came with a price. That price was to go back into the crevices of the GCSE route, and there was a caveat that came with that decision, I had to get at least an A or B+ in Maths and English.

This is required of someone who just turned thirty-eight years old, and considering the context and background of where I was coming from, this would be a juicy topic for saloon gossip if the results were shambolic. But that's the cross I have decided to hurl over my back. When marching towards a goal, one must acknowledge that it comes with its requirements. What makes it fun is when one is doing something radical at an age when most are releasing their legs off life's speedy pedal. I emulated the marathon runners who knew the same diet they would take to ensure they finished the race within a particular time.

When I decided to take that exam, I knew that I would need to rev up my studying but it wouldn't be the same kind of studying as when with my previous two degrees. I used to follow along with my classmates and try to keep up, but this exam would be new.

This plan was something radical because it was different from what most people around me were doing at my age. It's hard to get older and stay young, but it's even harder to decide that you will do something significant with your life when you're barely out of your 20s. It's one thing if you're an adult who's managing a home and working a job. It's another thing entirely if you're young enough that you feel like you've still got years ahead of you for things like having kids or making your fortune–but still old enough that you feel like there might not be enough time left for all the things you want to do before adulthood puts the brakes on your dreams.

I didn't think much about how it would feel when I started studying again–it was more about how it would feel once the studying paid off and I passed the exam. To pass the exam, I needed to act. I designed a plan which entailed studying for some hours daily, and this made me feel like a child learning how to walk again. There are some days that the walk seems to be going well, and some days where I would tip over because the stack reality of life was dealing new blows.

I had to look for a way to ensure that the household was held together–that involved the inflow of income. This brings me to my definition of luck. Some people would argue that luck is that shy lady that walks to you when you least expect her to show up. However, throughout this phase, I have come to the truth that luck is a lady that you call with your daily actions. If there were no actions to lure her into your courts, she would remain a shy lady staying in the distance. I have learned the importance of daily actions. This realisation is empowering, and it helps me build character as it provides me with a sense of responsibility for my happiness.

Actions are my new philosophy. They are the foundation of everything I do every day. My success depends on my action-driven life; without them, nothing could be achieved. My actions define me and my path in life. It's not just about taking action but having set goals, and direction are part of what makes it powerful.

The past few years were filled with self-doubt and indecision, but through self-realisation and introspection, I have discovered what needs to be done to reach my goals and dreams.

There are times that I thought that the fact that I was a Christian and a powerful speaking-in-tongues woman, that luck would continually dance in my space. The reality remains that life is a puzzle, and the onus lies on us to be able to piece them together.

To get further insight into healthcare, I started my first paid job with the National Health Service (NHS) as a 111-call handler on a part-time basis, along with my forty-hours-a-week job as a contracting Revenues and Benefits Assessor while studying for my GCSE at the same time.

What made the NHS 111 job even grander was the exposure it granted me to see what it meant to appreciate my existence as a human being. There was a lesson to learn from individuals who live but consider themselves dead–they struggled with mental health but still try to overcome those thoughts daily by taking minor positive steps. Whatever would make human life on both edges amazes me, and I drew positive lessons from the experience. Starting from the beginning, I gave free rein to the virtues of a new student with an inexhaustible repertoire to studying daily, which included studying six days a week while maintaining family and work pressure.

If possible, a good number of us would have escaped the daily grind of existence, but our why keeps keeping us–it keeps telling us to hold on and keeps pushing us to act in minuscule but meaningful ways. This journey is called life. When we are small, we're told to dream big and work hard to achieve our goals. But how many of us do that? How many of us can say that we do everything in our power to fulfil our dreams? A lot of us feel like we're spinning our wheels at times, treading water, and just barely getting by. We may have big plans, but we don't necessarily act on those dreams in a way that gives them the best chance of becoming a reality. But why is it so hard to push through sometimes? Why is it so tricky to progress toward our goals when we have them?

Many experts today believe that the problems arise because too much emphasis is placed on dreaming big but not enough on taking action. They say that people are led to believe that it's all about the end goal without understanding that it's the journey along the way that makes life worth living.

Working within the health sector created an ideal climate for me. The opportunity to discuss with patients rejuvenated the need to be thankful for my current position. I spent my free time and almost all my time ensuring that I soaked these stories and used them as the spur to act consistently. I cannot forget one story where the man had seven houses in the North of London, thirty-five chains of restaurants scattered around England, plus a beautiful family, and yet, he thought of exiting earth. He understood the essence of acting and executing excellently well. He mentioned that the story of life is much more than acting and argued that our actions must be driven by a divine purpose–not money, not material gains.

In essence, the rigorous training I was exposed to in the medical space and understanding how the systems could be used to save life-threatening situations corresponded in general to the vocation and nature of my divine purpose–my why. In these spaces, I deduced that my actions, no matter how little, became something that spurred me on.

Sometimes we wait to find motivation, for that morning sun to shine differently, and for the weatherman to announce that it is safe for us to go out. However, through this phase, I discovered that it is the periods of taking action that we find that motivation. Cal Newport, in his book, *So Good You Can't Be Ignored*, reminded us that passion is erratic. Still, the daily combination of action in a particular field can elevate that dead spirit in every individual. In short, he says: 'Find a job you love, and you will never work a day in your life.'

Finding a job you love is a difficult task if you have not found something that makes your heart beat faster and feels lighter, as if you are standing on top of the world. Many people spend their lives searching for something they love to do but end up wasting time looking for it. They don't realise that what they are doing connects them with some emotions and sensations related to their interest.

It happens pretty often that we do stuff without even knowing why or what for. We live without being conscious of what we are doing at every moment or looking for something we like without realising it's right under our noses. It might sound weird, but many people do precisely this. They forget about themselves and survive from one day to another, from one pay-check to another, from one social event to another.

In today's world, where we are surrounded by thousands of distractions and a lot of noise from social media, it is easy to lose focus on what we want to do. We get confused with thousands of ideas, professional and personal goals that we want to pursue but end up not doing so. Some people believe that the secret behind success lies in the passion for what you do.

As the very first step to kick-start your passion, Newport suggests you should "pick up a job you love." His theory deeply persuades us, and it's been repeatedly proved by many successful people who started as amateurs and eventually became masters at what they do.

As we all know, most professionals require years of practice before they fully achieve their expertise and become famous or influential enough to make a living out of what they love. What often comes as a surprise is that even experts need a solid start to develop their talent. Even those successful individuals you admire the most had to start from somewhere. But how did they get started? They found an entry point–a place to put down roots and begin their journey. They found something they could practice daily without losing their individuality and passion.

I became so spontaneous in my role that at the end of each day, I usually went home with an internal show of jubilation. It was not the lifesaving or the medical contribution; it was the fact that I had the opportunity to learn deeply about human existence. Meanwhile, the ultimate GCSEs waited while I slugged in sixty work hours.

It took a while and a structured approach to pass the exam. But, on the first attempt, I flunked it. I don't think there was a way to describe how I felt. Upon investigation and personal review, I found out that the hours poured into the sixty-hour job eliminated the study time, and this drastically told on my GCSE performance.

During that time, I was also fascinated by the offers hurled at me by various job agents, and here I was, trying to move forward in a new career. I thought it was a trajectory inspired by my mission to act. I slowly realised I was spread too thin and needed to concentrate on being more and not doing so much. Besides, passing GCSE would determine if I could gain admission to a UK medical school or not.

So, when I got offered a higher-paying contract by an agency, I turned it down not because it wasn't great and not because it wouldn't be an excellent opportunity, but because it didn't align with what I wanted to be doing. Saying *no* to that job helped me to get clear on what I wanted to be doing.

The poet, Maya Angelou, admonishes us to "continue to be bold, courageous. Try to choose the wisest thing, and once you've chosen the wisest thing go out and try to achieve it. Be it." The struggle, therefore, was how I could *be it.* We know to act, but sometimes we need to be bold and focus on becoming–a process with ups and downs.

My downs are as follows: I turned down a lot of jobs with mouth-watery offerings, over seventy percent drop in personal and a significant thirty-eight percent drop in household income, and tuning off a social life. I know I was supposed to be super optimistic about these bold decisions that I made to reach my dreams finally but to be honest, it was more complicated than I thought. I had a lot less money and a lot more uncertainty. Feelings of insecurity arose, and I wondered if my dreams were aligned with my reality.

This profound change in daily existence points to the reality of acting to become a new self. I did away with the routine of the past and formed new habits that would allow me to become unique. The new style set me on my path to becoming, reaching, and achieving what seemed impossible. The sacrifice must be weighed against the goal.

To build a house, one must first consider certain things in ensuring the building cost, the land, and other miscellaneous cost. While considering the time to act, one must first consider all the necessary items to ensure that all mitigating factors towards achieving that new feat is possible. This entails understanding why you want to do what you wish to, considering the goal, and eliminating all aspects that might deviate the individual from attaining that goal. One does not need motivation; what one needs is a disciplined approach.

Everyone has goals, and everyone wants to achieve those goals. But what happens when you don't know why you want to achieve the goal? Wouldn't that make the goals unachievable? A person lacking motivation will always lack discipline, self-control, and focus. This can be seen in someone who burns the midnight oil, works around the clock, or takes on tasks that are often great but overwhelming. The person is doing everything they can to achieve their goals, but they don't know why they want to achieve those goals in the first place.

The two main factors that are needed for success are motivation and knowledge. Without knowing what motivates you and how to reach your goal, how can you expect to succeed?

It is essential to be aware of what exactly you want, but it is also important to recognise what may stand in the way of achieving your goals. Certain factors may prevent you from reaching your plan that you may not even be aware of. For example, there could be an emotional factor, such as anxiety or stress, that is preventing you from performing your best.

One can set a goal and yet, not achieve that goal because of unforeseen circumstances. Outside of uncontrollable circumstances, I firmly believe that any goal can be achieved. The onus is on individuals to give up the magnificent ideology that any purpose is too tall to be reached.

Whether it's a new year or a decade, the time is ripe for goals. The start of a new year is an ideal time to make resolutions–resolutions that can be anything from health related to career related to relationship related. You can make anytime of the year the start of a new year for your goals; it does not have to be the 1st of January. Setting these goals and taking steps towards achieving them makes you feel empowered and ready to tackle the world.

Regarding the latter, I have always avidly believed in reaching a goal. Humans are masters at adapting to various circumstances and never giving up during hardship. I love how we constantly go through life-changing experiences yet somehow adjust and continue. Whether it's a career struggle or a relationship issue, we learn from our mistakes and move on more robustly than before. There are times when goals can be thwarted by outside forces–such as the death of a loved one, an illness of ourselves, or someone close to us–but I firmly believe that any goal can be achieved with determination and consistency.

I moved into the mentality which helped me cut away excesses like shopping for clothes, having exotic lunches or dinners, and celebrating birthdays in lavish style. This phase of my life, albeit heavy with its demands, presented a gift of appreciating other approaches to existing in life.

We all go through phases like this when we feel that we're just doing things because that's how everyone else does them, and we think it's what we should do. But if you've lived in this mindset for a long time, you know it can have drawbacks. For one thing, it can warp your sense of what you enjoy and don't enjoy doing–not to mention the self-consciousness that often goes with dressing up in specific ways or conforming to certain styles. After a while, something inside me said, "enough," and I began looking inward and outward for relief from these feelings.

I found some of my answers in the world of personal development. The most meaningful tool I found was limiting my wants to needs, which made me realise that there were plenty of things I didn't need but wanted. It helped me recognise how easy it is to get caught up in the whirlwind of envy surrounding us all the time. For a long time, I was a slave to a routine that revolved around the need to always have the best in life. I was living in a world of "more," where more money, more clothes, more shoes, and more food were synonyms for happiness. More turned out to be not necessarily better. So, I made another sacrifice–I started living on less, and I made myself believe that less is more.

Toward the end of the series of sacrifices, I passed the GCSE and was able to apply for medicine, and I was granted a space to study medicine. There are many lessons learned on this journey, but one that keeps me going even today is that goals are mere wishes if not backed up by actions.

If you're trying to take that leap, ask yourself why, calculate the cost, and act now. There is no need for coaxing your fingers or springing from an opposing couch of emotions. You must work and do it from a positive foundation. You too can!

NEW LEVELS.
NEW DE. VILS.

I never could have anticipated the "devils" patched into my new path. Above all the excitement it seems to me there is a concrete misplacement of what transpires when one elevates in any spectrum in life. At the age of forty! When my mates were either settling into a job or focusing on their family, I was on a journey to becoming a medical doctor.

I was not prepared for the challenges that were to come with this new phase in my life. I had no idea what it would take to be successful in medical school, let alone being able to handle all of life's ups and downs that come with such an endeavour. Throughout the next several years, I worked hard and experienced trials and tribulations that tested every part of my being. If you are in a similar situation as me and have decided to pursue your goals at an older age, I want you to know that you can do it!

But here is my take on it, from a perspective not often heard. The pursuit of self-actualisation often requires us to leave behind many of our previous relationships and attachments in order to pursue our passions and dreams. It is not uncommon for people who have achieved some level of success to find themselves feeling isolated and lonely, even when surrounded by people who love them.

The purpose of this book is not where I came from, but how I made it through tough times and how you can do the same!

One thing I didn't do in this journey was to analyse the devils waiting in these new levels. Often, I have maintained that positive mindset fuelled by green faith that the world from now is my oyster, that I too would carry the label of being a doctor in no short time.

I was super focused on the end goal and not the in-betweens, which would later rear its head in drips. The strangest thing is that I remained in the journey. I thought that if I could just focus on the finish line, everything would work itself out. But what I learned is that it's all about the journey in its entirety: being present and mindful of each step along the way. The best thing you can do for yourself is to learn how to appreciate every single moment, no matter how big or small. That's what I did, and it changed my life!

My family members had learned about my success on gaining admission into medical school. They celebrated with me, and the celebratory bottles were popped. The day finally came when I would be on the journey into this new era.

It is one thing to be excited about something that is coming your way, but it is another thing altogether to be able to maintain a calm head when the stakes are so high. I am unsure how much of a good job I did trying to maintain a calm head about the thought of starting medical school. I tried.

It was a surreal feeling, as if I was floating above my body and looking down at myself in that moment. My eyes were fixed on my reflection in the mirror and the tears streaming down from their faces seemed endless. The fears of failure started to creep up on me again. In my head, a strong string of lines was flashing like lightning and my mind was bubbling with thoughts about what to expect, how to behave and how to excel. Even more; I was worried about coping after a twelve-year academic gap.

Still, after doing these mind calculations, we embarked on that journey towards my university. Flashes of that ride comes to mind even today–the crisp paper smell of the air, the clear blue sky with its touches of white light and the gentle bounce the car did to our destination.

As a kid, I was drawn to new experiences and love to explore unknown fields. But for the most part of this experience, the fantastic details hung in between what to expect and what to be shocked by. My best resources of inspiration came from knowing that my family was fully behind me and from the faith I strongly hold in God.

At ten years old, I was already able to go out on my own and meet new people. I was surrounded by a lot of responsible adults who had given me their trust and so much support that it became easy for me to develop confidence as a person. The confidence that comes with knowing that you are loved by your family is definitely one of the things that helped me grow up into an independent person who knows how to make decisions on her own.

As a kid, I saw myself as someone who would always be searching for answers and inspiration until I found my purpose in life. Now that I'm older, however, I realise that there are no right or wrong answers when it comes to making choices about your future or even your present situation at hand. Your life is a gift, and you deserve to live it to the fullest–doing whatever you love the most.

First day, I moved into my student rented accommodation which was a gentle five-minute walk to the medical school. It was an en-suite living with a tiny bed, a brown desk, a single chair, and a reading lamp. I soaked the whole environment like a sponge and then it struck me, this is the new reality that I've signed up for. There was no going back!

At times I did not know how to manage the thoughts tugging at my mind. I had a strange feeling in my gut. It was a feeling that I had never experienced before. It was like a tug-of-war between my mind and my heart. On one side, my mind kept opening the can, showing me the struggles that laid ahead and at other times, it kept flashing positive visions of the green end goal.

This is a tip for the matured mind considering embarking on my journey. Your mind will play tricks on you and sometimes you would question your decision. Is this worth it? Yes, these are the quandaries that the mind will spring up at any given moment when one is embarking on something new. The great Hamletian question: *to be or not to be?*

The truth is, when embarking on a journey, there will be moments when it seems like everything is pointless–and that's okay! It's normal for your mind to question things. It just means that you are thinking critically about what you want out of life. And if you're willing to embrace this critical thinking process and not let it get in the way of your goals, then I promise that it won't be long before you start seeing results from all of your hard work!

And to make it interesting, this was a student accommodation and of course, that came with its attending characteristics. Young students wanting to enjoy their university days, partying hard, making silly noises during the small hours of the morning and leaving dirty dishes in kitchen sink. As a matured student this annoyed me to a great level, but I forgot in the instance that this was what student living was made from and here I was forgetting that I have retraced my steps to become a student again.

One thing, in retrospect, I should have got my own private apartment. This turned out to be one of the things I didn't consider–living in school apartment. I really did live that student life. Left to my husband, he would have loved to change the miniscule room into a five-star hotel as he wanted us to fit it with a nice little fridge, a new curtain, at least something to elevate the living standard. But I delivered a deafening silence to his admonition. I had more to worry about and they would unfold themselves gradually.

These are some of the accoutrements of new levels. The devil is in the passage into the new existence. Once you start unpacking the details of this new path, you begin to understand that there will be storms and there will be uncomfortable moments. From the very first day, these things began to unveil themselves. But then you start to see that your self-awareness is growing by leaps and bounds. You're becoming more and more aware of who you are and what you want out of life, and it's empowering. It's like finally having a map to guide you through the wilderness–a map with directions on how to get through each day, how to make decisions, how to keep yourself on track. You may have noticed that your life has changed dramatically over the past few days, but you are still learning how to adapt to these changes. As much as it may seem like everything is different now, it's not all bad! You can learn how to embrace this new life and find happiness within it if you work at it!

You may be feeling a little lost at this point in time. That's okay! Just remember that life is always changing and if you allow yourself to adjust to those changes with grace and gratitude for what is good about them, eventually you will find yourself in a place where everything feels right again. I cannot imagine sharing a dirty kitchen with kids half my age, but the reality of student living flashed before me like a jack in the box.

I began my school routine as a student and discovered another chilling truth. I was the oldest in my cohort. That made me feel like an aunt amid some little kids. I was not aware that during the splendour of this new experience, age was nothing but a number. The kids addressed me as they deemed fit and I made sure that I played the students life by chatting, learning their little innit-cum-young language just to blend in and managed to squeeze in a little time to be an emotional guide too.

In the beginning, I was not aware that age would be a factor in my school life. It wasn't until I started walking around campus that I realised that there was something different about me from my colleagues. They were all so young, almost like little kids with their giddy giggles and energetic bodies running around everywhere–but then there was me, who was almost twice as old as most of them.

I didn't want to think about it too much because I wanted to enjoy my new experience without feeling old or out of place, but it bothered me nonetheless. So, while they were busy chatting away with each other or playing games in class, I would sit back and try to learn their language by imitating them (or at least trying to). And then when everyone else had gone home for the day, I'd stay behind alone in the classroom to read or write alone until it was time for bed again, and then repeat it all over again the next morning.

Now, I have decided to take some steps back to unlearn what I knew about age and the dynamics of mingling with young adults. This level exposed me to the skills of dealing with individuals who thought the world revolved around their expectations. In effect, there was no confrontation coming my way as I soon realised that the only difference between them and me was that we had different sets of experiences, different relationships with our parents and different opportunities presented to us at different times in our lives. They were just kids who wanted to have fun while they were still young enough to do so. They had no worries about what would happen next, who would marry whom or who will take care of whom when they aged. They just needed someone who would listen to them without judging them for what they did not know yet. And this really opened up my eyes to the fact that we all have our unique way of living our lives irrespective of age or any other factor. We all have our own personality traits which make us who we are and it doesn't matter if we are young or old, young at heart or old at soul; what matters is how we choose to live our life.

I learned that navigating these waters meant understanding how to flow. Then again, on the flip side, I noticed that my personality began to sip out. My personal identity–because I thought blending in was the best approach–suffered.

In the classes, I wanted to be accepted by the environment and I didn't focus on redefining my inside man to meet the external presentation. As such, everything I began to do was like trying to fit a square in a circle. It made me learn that when one is entering a new level there is the need for a little self-assessment.

It is important to ask oneself, who am I? What will this new experience do to the self? How should I navigate this? At every little space, one should assess whether one is losing the self or allowing external factors control one. It is the ability to have these conversations within that would enable one face the devils outside.

I didn't have these self-talks and allowed myself to be blown by the wind of a new level. In time, I learned this fact: it is very nice to blend in but know thyself.

Classes started. I was the first in class. I never missed a beat. I came with the intuition from previous work and school experience, that it is better to be early. I walked into the room full of cleanliness, and there was the tutor, a young woman probably in her late twenties or early thirties.

Excited, I greeted her. I always regretted my tall excitement on that day because of the response she dished to me. I don't know if blaming her was the right thing to do or I should focus on myself. After greeting her, she muttered something under her breath, "this is the suck-up." Until then I had thought school was a place where every student and teacher aligned to ensure we were all successful, but this moment shook me back to reality. Expectations and reality in a new horizon differ greatly.

I sat down, saw my mind trying to form some gentle curses but I was able to redirect it to something positive. Maybe she was having a bad day, but that day remain affixed in my mind.

In the classes at the university, here at least, students and teachers exchange what we call respectable banter. A student can disagree with a teacher's logic of argument if the student can back up her premise. However, that Nigerian culture of showing excess respect to the teacher and not being able to question them was something that pushed me into having what seemed like excessive monologues in various classes. Instead of asking the tough questions about what I didn't understand, I allowed it slide. I didn't want to be classified by classmates as the "mama" of the class who found it hard to understand anything.

Having been scarred by that experience with the first tutor on the first day of my class made it complicated for my first year in school. I carried that scar like a badge of honour. This made my devotion to the merits of medical school suffer. It led to boredom.

I would find myself in classes and wished that the class ended immediately it started. There was a particular time when I wanted to put my tail in between my legs and return home. To put it simply, I wanted to quit.

Above all those negative emotions, I realised that the words I was feeding myself was fuelling negative actions and other nasty thoughts brewed in the back of my being. I asked myself, was I meant to be here? What are my mates doing now? In time I achieved a close affinity with these existentialities characterised by the unwillingness to be assiduous in my studies. Class became a chore.

These were the devils that accompanied this new journey. Without a doubt, I did not see this coming.

Even if I did see this coming, was there a way for preparing for this? I think for every new level that one enters, there is that challenge lurking in the corner. What matters is not what comes out of the corner, it is how we navigate those blows thrown unexpectedly at us.

I was not prepared for this feeling of wanting to run away from the very thing that I had always dreamed about doing. However, instead of running back home, I took a deep breath and decided that quitting wasn't the answer. Instead, taking a step back and looking at what was happening around me helped me realise that there were many things in life that were out of my control, but there were some things that were within my control and those were the only things worth focusing on.

In starting all over, it is not unusual for life to throw some blows; managed well, like a good boxer, we can weave them and throw punches back. Mismanaged, those blows can send us to the ground.

I decided after some good months of allowing my emotions deal me with some punches to walk out of that cauldron. It was time to find out how to study right and prepare for exams. I decided to find excellent students, study how they study and create a study group with them. I was straying again into the acceptance mode in the search of excellence. All my attempts failed, and I think fair enough to these students, my old-school approach towards studying was too boring for them. I started reading books on effective learning and motivational psychology, but nothing worked for me. The problem was that I didn't know what worked well for me yet, so it was hard to know what kind of methods would be effective in getting me prepared for exams.

I had to accept that I was not their ideal student and they were not mine either. They wanted something different from me, something new and exciting. I had to accept that there is no one way of studying that works for everyone. We all have our own learning styles and preferences when it comes to studying. I had to accept that what worked for me in high school may not work as well at university level. I had to accept that there are other ways of studying than mine and other ways might be better suited for me than my old school methodologies.

I had never faced failure before (as much as I could), but this failure made me realise that if you don't accept things for what they are and keep looking for the perfect solution, then you will never be able to move on or grow as an individual.

As my formative exam in the first year drew near, I mustered all the energy I could to prepare in the right way. I created a timetable which meant studying after classes, cramming some areas I thought were tough, and resting as little as possible. This preparation took away my hair like a bad barber. My fondness for being wanting to be the best student splashed a rude awakening in my face. I failed!

I sat there wondering how it had happened to me? Where did I go wrong? Why did this happen? All these questions kept popping up in my head and no answers came forth. All I could do was stare blankly into space with tears welling up in my eyes because of the dense sadness in my heart.

I don't know if it was the first encounter I had with the teacher. I don't know if it was me trying to fit into the group and I don't know if it has to do with the age gap. But I know one thing for sure, I didn't sit-down to count the cost of this level. I didn't carry out a thorough analysis of what was to come. And to back that up, the head tutor made it clear that matured students like me with little science background usually found it hard in their first couple of months in study and gave me that positive closing: 'you will excel if you put in the extra work, and you will be a brilliant doctor.'

Those words washed away the experience and set me on a pedestal where I told myself that I would not allow negatives control me in this new level. I took the result home and decided to hatch a plan that would allow me to achieve the results needed to excel in this new level.

LIFE IS FOR LIVING

I could hardly believe my ears–she seemed so lively and full of energy–and just like that she was no more. The wind of life blew her to the other side of existence. As always, we can't predict the tune life will play but how we play life will determine the type of music we would be remembered by.

I remember my friend, she splashed her pink colours all over the earth. When she came into your life you could smell her adventurous self and when she opened her mouth you wanted to see the world through her eyes. She lived more than fully–she would attend parties, dress impeccably without forgiving her colour mixes and smiled always. I do not think I felt in the least repressed about her sojourn to other side of existence.

For me, it was more of a lesson about living. Even at forty, I think she lived more than six scores wrapped in one life. And here I was enmeshed in the pursuit of one educational achievement and forgetting the essence of life.

As I rolled in the medical muddy journey, I began to allow life and existence ebb away. It began gradually. The art of pursuit of a goal and the actual experiencing of life while in pursuit are extremely two different things. For me, I started noticing some fat hanging out in the wrong side of my body and I realised a walk that would have taken at least five minutes to complete was taking almost double that time. Is this what is expected of me as a student? Is this not what it is expected to be? To become this slow and heavy woman who would come out after some months here with a degree to show but without her health intact. Is this not the sacrifice? The sacrifice that I must become a medical doctor, and this is the battle scar that I will show. These questions formed a ball in my head, and I carried this thought around for a while.

But then the reality comes to my mind that life is for the living. When I say this, I am not saying that one should engage in life with an attitude of no guidance or no structure or no defined goal. I am saying that those who achieve great feats also must learn to live. I decided to take care of my health, after all what type of doctor would I be if I am struggling at this young age to walk short distances without tasting my lungs in my mouth.

I enrolled in the gym with the intention to exercise not for the proverbial six packs but to at least engage in other things while on the journey to becoming a medical doctor.

I think for most people who have the faith and are determined to achieve a goal, there is that tendency to pack most things by the side and focus on that goal. That's a good way to go but what usually transpires is that we forget to live. We forget about the vessel that is embarking on that journey and what the vessel needs.

As someone who has lived through such an experience, I know how easy it is for your mind to be so occupied with achieving success that you forget about everything else. In my experience, some of us tend to forget about our health while we focus on our goals. We spend so much time working on our business plans or other things that will get us closer to achieving our dreams, which sometimes means we neglect ourselves.

The vessel is you. The vessel is your body, mind and soul. The vessel is also your family, friends and community. You cannot forget about them as well or else you will end up feeling miserable, frustrated and unhappy which will cause you to lose focus on your goal.

You can still achieve your goals while being mindful of the needs of others around you because it allows you to appreciate them more which helps you reflect on what they mean in your life and how they have impacted it positively or negatively over time.

You need to eat well, sleep well, and exercise. If you don't do these things, your body won't be able to keep up with the demands of your journey. You'll get sick or injured, and then what are you going to do?

A ship setting sail on a treasure hunt still needs the right fuel, needs the crew, and needs steering. So, you must fuel your ship the right way and failure to do so can lead to extreme boredom and lethargy.

I witnessed the boredom part immediately I had that experience with that teacher who shooed me away in my first day at school. I withdrew like a snail back into her shell and kept to myself most of the time. I noticed that I was slowly turning into something strange. I became a stranger to my real self, and I was allowing the whole situation to control my existence. I forget exactly when it was that my husband told me to snap out of the situation. The only way for me to achieve this was to be my natural self. What would my natural self do about this situation?

One evening when the sun was taking a gentle stroll into the night, I mustered what till today were the contours of my own existence–the courage to settle things. I headed to the office of that teacher and rolled out the pains she caused me on her table. I noticed that she was about to drown in the description I poured out and she apologised in such a way that made me feel proud. These are the little things about living your life.

There are areas that we know that would prevent us from living our lives fully and yet we allow other things slow us down. Sometimes it could be fear to become something new while on that journey and we lie about the goal.

Neglect is the name of the game I began to play. Things like taking care of myself took the back seat. All I thought about was this goal. But these things lead to a burnout and the monotonousness of the hall-of-residence-school-library regime drained beauty out of me. There was no time, I thought, for me to engage in any frivolous activity. I want to become a doctor! All other things must be vanity. And that's where I got it wrong.

I know that it's easy to feel like you're the only person out there who has these kinds of issues, but trust me–you're not. I've been there too! And what I've learned is that it's not just about getting over your fear or finding a way to get rid of the negative habits you have; it's about learning how to love yourself for who you are and respecting your body for what it does for you every day.

We all have days when we feel like we should be doing more or eating better or exercising more–and those days can make us feel like we're failing at life. But the truth is, no one is perfect! You don't have to be "perfect" in order to be happy and healthy, and if you can learn to accept yourself exactly as you are (even when times are hard), then everything else will fall into place.

One morning I looked in the mirror and called my name three times as if I wanted to talk to myself. There was nothing new the mirror told me. I only heard it saying those words: 'life is for the living. I want to become a doctor!'

The mirror spoke: 'you are now looking like an ordinary piece of work. Where is your beauty? Did you hear that those who are on the journey to become doctors are usually this unkempt? When was the last time you went to the saloon? Why are you allowing this journey to reshape the person that you are? Can't you live and be a good student at the same time?'

That year, I did some of the things I always wanted to do. I got my afro dyed in gold and bought a brand-new red spectacle. At least, with this, I added colour to myself.

The most important thing about the body is, the amount of care we pour into it is what it uses to fuel the soul. The trio of body, soul and mind still come to play no matter what journey one is embarking on.

When I splashed those colours on my face, I noticed two important things: I began to feel energy within me to conquer the course with fun and I began to appreciate my existence on campus more. I started off by doing a research about colours and their effects on the mind. In fact, there are studies that show that wearing red increases productivity and creativity. This could be because red is a colour that evokes strong emotions such as passion and anger.

In addition, blue has been proven to slow down mental processes which can help us focus better on our work. It also helps us feel more relaxed and peaceful, which is great for students who are always under stress due to deadlines or exams. Scientific studies have shown that yellow makes people feel happy and optimistic about life in general, which is why it's often used as a safety colour in construction sites or hospitals where patients need to feel safe or relaxed while they recover from an illness or injury.

Green is known as the colour of nature because it stimulates growth and vitality in humans, which explains why we often see green being used as a calming colour in hospitals because it helps reduce anxiety levels among patients.

I used this knowledge for my own benefit–to awaken the feminine side of myself that I have been neglecting for months before.

What one must consider is living in a way that represents one to the fullest because this is what confidence is made of. One of the great joys of these new self was–I became adventurous–I took on swimming.

Swimming, dear reader is a good exercise that has the magnificent capacity of working the whole body. After a couple of laps in the water, the rejuvenating energy could allow one feel great. And the thing about this is it didn't affect my work and only motivated me to feel more focused.

There is this lie that most people tell themselves that they must suffer to achieve a goal but sometimes, we can live a little in the pursuit of our goals.

In the case of books, and the general luxuries of basking in stories, there were some of those that kept my world sane, and they are *The Power of I am* by Joel Osteen, *Commanding Your Morning* by Cindy Trimm and *The Power of Positive Confession* by Matthew Ashimolowo. These were rich worlds that I could enter, and they reminded me of the possibilities that could still be derived from existing with infinitely more advantages. Through these books, I was able to understand the role of having positive affirmations and pronouncing them daily.

Positive affirmations were like the serving of the first meal of the day for the soul. I cannot think of any other meal the soul needs daily than these daily mantras. Try it and see the magic it can do for your life.

Another thing most people do is that they eliminate relationships while walking in these journeys. What most forget is that maintaining a healthy relationship can make or destroy all the effort that has been poured into the journey.

In reality, despite the many stories and movies that tell us otherwise, we live in a society that has trained us not to believe in ourselves. Instead, society has taught us to think in specific social narratives and attain those narratives. How many movies depict the notion that we must continue until we defeat the bad guy to become a champion or that we must date a large number of different partners before we discover the perfect one? Half of the difficulty is the framework that is being established. Perseverance is essential, but it must be combined with the courage to follow your heart. Maybe you don't need a love partner for the rest of your life. Perhaps you don't need to be conquering other fellas or being a champion of anything.

Start peeling away the layers of ego by looking at all the stories that are tugging the strings on you. And if you have no idea what's in your heart, you're much more lost and vulnerable to societal deception. I can't tell you how many people believe that following one's heart isn't "practical" since it won't earn "money" or something like that. Some of you who have followed your passion and made a living doing so understand how much of deception this is, but societal conditioning is ingrained in us all. Every day, countless people ignore their emotions in favour of following the path they believe would keep them safe or gain them the most social acclaim, which is at best a watered-down version of ego-love. As you progress, you'll encounter a lot of preconceived notions about what love is.

You'll have to confront your beliefs about yourself and your deservingness of love. People don't believe in themselves for various reasons, one of which is that they don't believe they are deserving of love. The good news is that you are the only one who can make a difference. And that's liberating because you can always have your love, regardless of how anyone else feels about you. You can't go too far without rethinking everything in many respects. You'll discover that your assumptions are incorrect as you examine them. You are deserving of love. You are worthy of belief. You can follow your heart in this lifetime and have your heart, body, mind, and soul taken care of.

Living life entails making plans with your loved ones to enjoy life. There are many stories on the internet that tells the woes of people who achieved great deeds and lost their families. I don't see that as living life fully. To me, I think those who win are those who can accomplish great feats with their loved ones still together and those who draw energy from the existence of their family unit. And family is not necessarily one of blood, it is those who stand with you through tough time and share your happiness

Arriving home from school every weekend was a joyous reunion. I enjoyed that weekend cookout and having to narrate the week to the patient listening ears of my husband and other family members. Our monthly budget was stretched by this weekly commute, but we managed to maintain it as this helped with my mental health.

Home is where the wealth is. I will never agree to the weekend requests to attend one party or something that would take me away from my family. It was in this period that I learnt about the strength of the family unit. I am not saying those who don't have this can't draw strength from other places; in fact, I did draw strength from numerous places. One such place was the church. Amidst commuting a long journey home, I still made time for the church. For me, this has always served as my spine. On the rock is where I have built my solid attitude to be better and to exist in the fullness of God's grace. Not to be too preachy here but anyone can do well if they tap from God's eternal grace. I assume it is already clear for you what the prescription of my heartache is, helping others. I do this because I know how hard it is to be alone in these times.

For me after every Sunday service, I was sure to have a good week. If you want to see how it works study the works of great men that have tapped strength from the Word of God.

All these poured into my academics and the result began to change. I noticed for the first time that I was eager to learn more and extract value from every class. There was this new glow I saw when I approached the mirror. It was too bright that sometimes I had to prevent it from blinding my eyes. I composed a few songs in my mind, setting some of the verses to speak about the importance of taking living life. It goes: "for those who see life as a playground, they should play and explore all the infinite possibilities."

Perhaps that could serve as your mantra, dear reader. Perhaps you could use that as a springboard to write your own daily mantra. Some of the things we want to achieve can be done simultaneously while with our lives. One can't be on a journey and forget about one's life. That's setting oneself for failure. Imagine a car without fuel, without headlamps, without breaks, and without servicing. That car would breakdown. If as humans we don't exercise, eat the right food, and enjoy the simple things of life then what we are trying to achieve becomes an illusion.

There is the saying that life is for the living but what does it mean to live? To live means to pay attention to three elements of being: the mind, the body, and the soul. The three are interwoven and only those who pour into these three features daily will achieve their goals. It is not enough for us to think that we want to achieve something, it is reaching the destination in good health, with those we love and with enough energy to enjoy the post-achievement part of the goal. I mean, what will it profit a soul if it reaches its goal and loses its own health?

THE MILLION GREY AREAS OF LIFE

Indeed, life isn't always black and white. How you handle the millions of shades in between is crucial in starting all over again. Yes, you need to make a change, but you also need to know that it's okay if you don't want to make a big leap right away. You can take smaller steps toward your goal without feeling like they don't count.

It's important to remember that everything in between the extremes of "I'm doing great" and "I'm doing terrible" is a spectrum. And the world isn't going to stop spinning just because you're not where you want to be yet.

You're not alone in this–everyone has shades of grey in their life right now. What matters is your willingness to keep moving forward in spite of them.

We all have days when we feel like life is black and white. The good guys are good, the bad guys are bad, and it's all pretty cut-and-dried. But then there are those other days when things just aren't so clear–when you're not sure what to think or feel about something, or how to react to it. And those days can be tough.

But here's the thing: what matters most isn't that you know exactly what you should do in every situation–it's that you have a system for handling those shades of grey, so that when you're not sure what to do, or how to feel about something, you can still move forward with confidence.

My 4th year of medicine was by far the most stressful for a combination of reasons. It is the year I of my final written exam and my performance in the 4th year of medical school goes a long way to shape the proceeding three years of my career–where I live and what speciality I work in.

Every UK medical graduate who wishes to work as a doctor undergoes a compulsory two-year foundation job post medical school to obtain your full GMC licence. Unlike most careers where fresh graduates can apply for jobs where they would want to live; in medicine your exam performance determines where you will end up in the UK. You could be a Londoner like me but end up with a foundation job in Scotland or Wales based on your exam scores.

Your ranking in medicals known as Education Performance Measure (EPM) in combination with the result from a national exam called Situational Judgement Test (SJT) would be used to determine how well you have done to end up in your desired location for foundation training.

I had lived away from home, from my husband for almost six years and did not want to risk another two years away, so I had to put everything I could to ensure I secured a foundation job near home.

I re-organised my schedule and minimised any distractions for those nine months to ensure I passed with my finals. I stayed off social media and social scenes for months, and would turn my phone off for hours to focus on study. This has now evolved into a habit for my mobile phone to perpetually be on silent mode to the annoyance of my friends and families as I often miss their calls. I am working to break this habit.

How do you organise your schedule and minimise distractions? I can give you some helpful tips straight from my own experience.

Plan the week.

Write down everything you need to get done, and make sure that it's realistic for the time frame you have available.

Plan your day, week and month. Your daily schedule should include meals and snacks, exercise time (if applicable), social engagements (if any), work hours or school/college class times–whatever has been decided upon by yourself or others as being important in your life right now.

Get up early!

The best way to start your day off right is by getting up early. When you wake up in the morning, there are no distractions and you can focus on what's important. If you have an alarm set, that means less time spent worrying about missing something important or forgetting something vital. You can also spend some time doing things like meditating, reading a book or journaling before anyone else is awake.

When starting this routine, it might take some time for your body to adjust–but once it does, waking up early will feel like second nature.

Prioritise what is important. For example, if weight loss is your goal, exercise and healthy meal should be your top priority. Likewise, if passing an exam is your goal, studying should be at the top of your to-do list.

Spend as much time on your priority. If it means missing out on social events, then you should! It's important that you prioritise the work that will help you achieve your goals in life and make a living for yourself.

Get good sleep. No phones.

Don't go to bed too late.

If you must have music playing, then make sure it's classical music, as opposed to pop music which has more of an upbeat tempo that can be distracting when trying to sleep and may cause you to stay awake longer than necessary as it's not conducive for sleeping.

Snack on healthy foods between meals, not junk food.

Plan spontaneous things with your friends and families during your down time. You don't necessarily have to plan ahead for this kind of thing–in fact, it can be more fun if you don't! Just make sure that whatever spontaneous activity or outing you choose doesn't require a lot of prep time (like going out to dinner), because then there will be less opportunity for procrastination later on in case something comes up during the day that prevents you from being able to leave right away (like getting caught up at work).

The takeaway is that you should start scheduling your day in advance so that you can minimise distractions and get things done. You also need to make sure that the schedule reflects your priorities, otherwise it won't work for you.

Finally, organise your schedule so that there isn't too much going on at once. This will help keep things organised and make sure nothing slips through the cracks.

My activities most days were study, pray, gym, eat, catch up on the news and talk to a few close friends and family. It was not easy but was necessary. I saw it as a temporary pain for a permanent gain.

Despite all this effort, it was almost as if some element of the universe rose up to oppose every effort. I kept finding myself in situations where I felt like I was getting nowhere, even though I was working as hard as possible. It felt like no matter how hard I tried, there was always something standing in my way.

It took me a long time to realise that these obstacles were actually part of the process–they were there because they had to be in order for me to succeed!

I started having different health challenges.

One was pain on the left side which kept me awake at night–I could not lie on the left side of my body for more than few minutes without experiencing burning pain and numbness in my upper and lower limbs. At first, I put it down to sciatica, but I knew within me that the symptoms were not keeping with sciatica, but I just was not ready to subject myself to a long process of investigations and differential diagnoses. I had a final exam to study for plus it would mean regular travel from the midlands where I was studying to my local hospital in the southwest.

The burning pain at night progressed to weakness in the limbs, which I had noticed, but was highlighted by my swimming instructor–she noted my right limbs were stronger than my left. The night-time pain started appearing in the day and my left eye started to blink on its own endlessly. Then I developed a bothersome kidney stone which was a source of constant pain on my left flank. This was in combination to chronic constipation which left me with painful fissures on defecation.

As if I did not have enough to deal with, after repeated inconclusive cervical smear, I was referred for colposcopy. At one point I was under the neurologist, the urologist, the colorectal surgeon, and the gynaecologist for different investigation.

Whilst the cumulative health challenges got in the way of study and got me overwhelmed, I recognised it as a spanner in the works and was more determined than ever to pass my finals. I also started managing some of the symptoms conservatively myself like drinking loads of water to manage the kidney stone as well as the chronic constipation.

The neurologist concluded that the symptoms were due to mental health issues from anxiety about exams and other events that had occurred in my life when I was a child which is laughable because this was not the case at all. This to me is the kind of doctor I do not want to be who make wrong diagnosis based on their biased opinion and not patient's presentation or who blames their inability to diagnose a symptom on mental health. He did one thing right though, by referring me for MRI of my brain to rule out multiple sclerosis.

I stuck to my study schedules as originally planned. Attended my hospital appointments and prayed–it is the only tool I have ever known to see me through tough times.

Different people engage different tools to see them through tough times. For some people, it would be taking on a new challenge to distract them, and to others it would be talking to a psychologist. For me it is prayer. Whatever works for you, use all you have to protect your mental health.

It's easy to get lost in the idea that we have to be strong, or that we can't let our guard down. But the truth is, sometimes it's okay to ask for help. I've been there. I know how hard it is to let yourself feel vulnerable and open up about what you're going through. But I also know that when you do, it can make all the difference in your recovery process.

For me, prayer has always been a huge part of my life–and it still is today. Over the years, I've found that prayer helps me keep perspective on things and remind myself why I'm doing what I'm doing. You should also find something, either a mental or physical activity, that will help you calm down and be in check with the reality.

By the time the exam came, I was so exhausted physically and mentally that I had gone beyond caring about my EPM ranking–I just wanted to pass enough not to repeat the year.

When my result came, instead of going to look for my score marks compared to my peers, all I looked out for was "progress to year 5." It would be days before I went back to peruse my result for my actual score and the breakdown of how I performed.

The truth is while we have the grand plan and clear goals on how to start again, the unexpected can happen. I have heard of cases of people who landed their dream job only to be diagnosed of cancer? Or lost a spouse at the birth of long-awaited pregnancy. What do you do?

Life is full of surprises and that's what makes it beautiful. These events might be painful, and they may not go according to our plan, but they are necessary in order for us to grow as human beings and become better people.

Whilst some people never recover from this stage of the process, some sail through.

The purpose of this chapter is to share the challenges I had when starting again and to offer hope to anyone who may feel stuck or overwhelmed on this journey.

KEEP YOUR WHY IN FOCUS

Me: 'Hello, Dad. How are you?'

Dad: 'I'm good, Dr Chris- Kuye.'

Me: 'I am not yet a doctor Dad, I am only just starting my final year of medical school. I have a few months to go before you can call me a doctor.'

Dad: 'Don't worry my daughter. You're already a doctor. By the way, you know those doctors that fixed the broken bones in my leg when I had the accident. I would like you to be one of them.'

Me: 'Oh, the trauma and orthopaedic surgeon. (Laughing quietly to myself) and managing to say okay just so we don't prolong the conversation and not to break his heart by telling him I would never become a trauma and orthopaedic surgeon.'

'Hold on for your mum.'

Me: 'Hello, Mum.'

Mum: 'Hello, doctor.'

Me: (Rolling my eyes). 'Mum. I am not yet doctor.'

Mum: 'How many babies have you delivered?'

Me: 'Mum, I'm just checking on you. I have to go now. Love you. Speak to you soon.'

When beginning again it is always good to begin with the end in mind. Otherwise, you can get side-tracked by a lot of things, people's opinions, people's advice. The end goal is what you should be focusing on at all times. You need to know where you are going before you can get there, right? And if not, how will you know where you are? The same goes for your goals and dreams. You need to know what they are before anyone else does or else how will you know if they have been achieved? And once again, if not, how will anyone see that it has been achieved?

Be mindful of your goals, and making sure that the things you do today will help you achieve them. Make sure your goals are realistic, achievable and measurable so that you can see progress towards them. Be sure to set deadlines for yourself so that once something is completed or achieved then there will be no reason for procrastination or disorganisation because every task has an end date next to it on your calendar!

So, when you are beginning again, remember that the end is what matters most. If you are not yet going towards your goal then at least try to be moving in a direction that helps you get closer to it!

Oftentimes, well intended, like my parents wanted me to be different doctors rolled into one. My mum wanted me to be an Obstetrics and Gynae (O&G) doctor. My dad wanted me to be an orthopaedic and trauma doctor. Or my spiritual dad wanted me to be a surgeon of any kind.

As much as I like most specialties in medicine, it is humanly impossible to be everything in medicine. There comes a time where you have to choose a path to go. Thanks to the rigorous self-assessment or self-evaluation that I did prior to starting medical school. I knew the speciality that my personality, skill set, and passion would be most suited to and everything I did in Med school was geared towards excelling in this speciality.

The truth is, I was tempted by other specialities that I enjoyed, especially obstetrics and gynaecology, and could probably make a success of it if I applied myself, but the question I ask myself is, *where would I be most fulfilled? Why did I decide to begin again by training to become a medical doctor?* What is my why?

My why is acute medicine/lifestyle medicine. Going to do O&G or trauma and orthopaedics will be going back to where I started from: living my parents' dream.

The closest people to you have the greatest influence on your life. They sometimes are hugely instrumental in shaping your personality, values, beliefs and dreams. They also help you set goals and achieve them. However, they will never live your life. We need our own experiences in order for us to grow as individuals and reach our full potential.

I was very conscious and intentional on keeping the end in focus at every stage of medical school. I paid a lot of attention in sharpening those skills needed for my speciality of interest and spent more time within those departments.

I knew I did not want to be a surgeon, so I would only go to the theatre when I was timetabled to be there, but would stay in A&E beyond my timetabled sessions. Similar to my GP surgery, I would expend myself far beyond the call of duty during my GP placement. I would join the GP society carrier, and carry out my elective in acute medicine. I would approach a doctor with a special interest in lifestyle and nutrition to be part of the group so I could deepen my interest in lifestyle medicine.

Whilst I listen and considered the options and advise presented to by friends, families, mentors and contemporaries, I was careful to stay focused on the reason I started.

Understanding my why served as a point of reference for my goals and kept me focused. They helped me stay on track on days when my motivation was dwindling.

SAVOUR THE SWEET TASTE OF SUCCESS

The long-awaited email to confirm my graduation ceremony has finally arrived.

Am I really prepared to be a doctor? I asked myself.

A feeling of trepidation swells up at the thought that I will be entrusted with looking after very ill persons in a few weeks. I would no longer be able to hide under the canopy of 'I am just a medical student.'

Have I been tried, tested, and deemed qualified to look after sick people? Very sick people? I asked again. This is classic imposter syndrome. I muttered to myself as I stood in front of the dressing mirror in our closet with a reflection of my graduation dress in the background.

I have written countless number of written and practical exams in the last seven years and managed to pass all except my finals OSCE which I had to resit. But despite these successes, I still struggled with imposter syndrome–that feeling of being a fraud who will be exposed at any moment for not having earned their accolades or achievements. This type of mindset is common among high-achieving individuals. Still, it can also affect anyone else who tends to be hard on themselves and beat themselves up over mistakes they make (even if they aren't mistakes).

Perfectionism is a symptom of imposter syndrome and can be caused by the fear of failure. Perfectionists are often afraid to try new things because they feel they won't be able to live up to their expectations or meet what others expect from them.

Imposter syndrome is a common phenomenon. This condition causes people to doubt their achievements and internalise fear of being exposed as fraud. It usually emanates from things like perfectionism and fear of success, and it takes a conscious and intentional change of mindset to overcome it.

If you are the type that wants everything done "right" or "perfectly" before moving on to the next stage or project in your life, you may be suffering from perfectionism and may usually suffer from imposter syndrome in your journey of starting all over again. While this can be beneficial at times (like when you're learning how to drive), it can also lead you down a path where there are no shortcuts or quick fixes–you must do everything perfectly every single time! This means that even if something goes well, but if there is room for improvement, this experience won't count towards building confidence because to a perfectionist, nothing will ever be perfect enough.

If you're suffering from imposter syndrome, it's important to remember that it is not uncommon. You are not alone, and there are many people out there who suffer from this same issue. However, it can be overcome with a change of mindset and some conscious effort toward understanding what drives the fear behind feeling like an imposter in the first place.

To avoid the adverse effects of imposter syndrome, you need to beat this mindset.

- Recognise that imposter syndrome is rooted in unhealthy perfectionism. Unhealthy perfectionism is counterproductive. You are bound to do something imperfectly.
- Pay attention to your thoughts. Stop comparing yourself to others. Do not let it hold you back.

I must have been having this internal conversation of not deserving my degree for about five minutes when I suddenly realised the tricks my mind was about to play on me and said out loudly, 'DT, stop it! You earned this degree–it has not just dropped on your lap. It is not a lucky break. It is not a fluke. You have worked hard for it.'

You ought to celebrate your success with yourself by yourself and with those who love you and those who have cheered you on for the last six years, and that was precisely what I did.

For many years, I have been doing a lot of things alone. I mean, it is not that I am antisocial. Many people taught me how to celebrate success and failure through their actions, theirs and mine. My husband in particular does an excellent job in magnifying my successes no matter how small. He would hold me in his arms and repeatedly say to me, 'I am proud of you.' He is also the first person I learnt how to communicate my failures to.

Although, with the miniscule doubts and intermittent injection of imposter syndrome in my mind, I wanted to be alone. I did not want to celebrate my graduation of becoming a doctor. However, I still decided that the best way to start a new chapter of my life is to create it with those who love me and those who have cheered me on for the last six years.

I gathered a trusted team with me. Event Planners, Caterers, MC, friends and families and I threw the best celebratory party ever to celebrate six years of hard work, diligence and commitment.

I laughed and danced so much that my joints were screaming for rest. I'd laughed and danced to celebrate six years of complex work, diligence, and commitment. Six years of sweat, tears, and blood.

Finally, part of savouring success is giving back. I did mine by mentoring a prospective medical student for free and offering my time to teach and sit on the interview panel for medical school admission. I also did charity events to raise money for medical research. However, giving back does not always need to be a grand gesture. The main thing is that you do not gatekeep your success, and you make sure to share your wisdom as much as possible. Use your passion to make the world a better place. It is simple as that!

BE THE GIFT THAT KEEPS GIVING

Now that you have achieved your dream in starting again–give back to the society. This is not just about getting recognition but also about giving back to the society in some way or another. When thinking about making an impact, think about what you can offer to the society.

Giving is one of the fundamental laws of success.

The thing you want to give back should be something that is close to your heart, and you can start from your little corner of the world.

You can give money, you can give your knowledge, your effort, your love. This can be done through anything from teaching, volunteering, or coaching or sponsoring young kids to helping people start up their own business or something as simple offering basic computer skills–anything to empower people to better themselves.

If you read books on wealth creation, giving is one tool that recurs over and over, so when you give, you are not only empowering and making other people's lives better, but you are also inadvertently creating wealth for yourself.

My way of giving back was to:

Offer my time to mentor prospective medical student.

Offer my time to teach medical students in preparation for their exams.

Offer my time to sit on interview panel for medical school admission (this was a paid service, but I chose not to pursue the payment for it).

I gave out my books from medical books for free or charge a small fee for postage.

For the medical books I sell, I donate the money to charities like Great Ormond Street Hospital Charity (GOSH).

Volunteer for self paid medical mission to developing countries with charity organisations.

I share my story of how I started again, not from a place of inflated ego or in a way to brandish my achievement or make anyone feel less, but to encourage and show people what is possible.

I hope my story and this book has inspired you to make a difference. The world needs more people like you, who are willing to give back and help others navigate the murky waters of life.

EPILOGUE

"The journey of a thousand miles begins with one step."

–Lao Tzu

I don't know about you, but I can't help but feel like this proverb is pretty much the most accurate thing ever. It's so true! If you want to start again, if you want to make a change in your life, something that's going to stick and make an impact for years to come, you're going to have to start somewhere. And if you're anything like me, in starting again, it can be hard to know where to begin. But trust me–you're not alone! And as long as you keep that first step in mind, you'll be able to keep moving forward until your dreams become reality.

So, get out there and do it! Start today! You'll never regret taking that first step towards what matters most (or at least if you do, it won't be forever). I believe that we are all capable of great things regardless of age, gender, creed or race. We all have the ability to change, grow, and give back.

I hope that this book has helped you find the strength to start all over again, follow your dreams and realise your potential.

I want to leave you with a few ideas for how you can keep moving forward:

- The first and most important thing I would like you to acknowledge and affirm is YOU ARE NOT TOO LATE TO START AGAIN, regardless of your age, gender, race or circumstance.
- Remember that there is life outside of your comfort zone. Your comfort zone is a wonderful place, but it's important to step out into the world every once in a while. "You cannot discover new oceans unless you have the courage to lose sight of the shore", in the words of Andre Gide.
- Write down the reason/s you decided to start again. Write down what you want to achieve. Write down how you want to achieve these things and let them serve as your vision board.
- Ask questions from those that are doing what you are planning to do. Be curious. Recognise the right source of help and seek timely help from them–we see more and farther when we stand on the shoulders of giants.
- Take steps each day (no matter how little) towards your desired goals.
- Be determined. Be consistent. Be diligent. It is almost impossible to successfully start anything new again without these three elements.
- Review your decisions and actions regularly to ensure they align with the reasons and actions on your vision board.

- To squash distractions and derailment, it is important to understand and constantly keep in my mind the reason you are starting again.
- Recognise there will be obstacles along the way; don't let them keep you down or truncate the journey of starting again.
- Celebrate successes (the big, the small and the in between). Learn from the failures.

In giving back, you don't have to be a celebrity, a politician or a social media influencer to make a difference in the world–you just need to be willing. You can start from your own little corner of the world. I hope this book has helped you find your own path to start again towards making a difference by recognising you are never too late to start again.

If it has, please take a moment today and share what you've learned with someone else. Tell them about how you're going to make a difference in the world and how they can too!

Thank you for reading and supporting me on my journey to become a better person.

I will love to hear from you. You can share your "never too late" story or journey with me via info@chronicless.org

Printed in Great Britain
by Amazon

26395788R00064